Music and Sound in the Healing Arts

Music
and Sound
in the Healing Arts

An Energy Approach

John Beaulieu

Station Hill Press

Published by Station Hill Press, Inc., Barrytown, New York 12507.

Produced by the Institute for Publishing Arts, a not-for-profit, tax-exempt organization in Barrytown, New York. Grateful acknowledgement is due to the National Endowment for the Arts, a federal agency in Washington, D.C., and the New York State Council on the Arts for partial financial support for the literary projects of Station Hill Press and the Institute for Publishing Arts.

Design and production by Susan Quasha and George Quasha. Production assistance, by Richard Gummere and Bryan McHugh. Staff assistance by Frauke Regan and Paul Woodbine. Outside consultation by Stephanie Tevonian of Works in New York City. Cover © 1987 by Susan Quasha and George Quasha.

Jacket photo of the author and photos of the author in the text are by Georgio Palminsino. Drawings and notations in the text are primarily by the author. Acknowledgements for other visual material and for citations in the text appear in the Notes on page 135 and are reprinted by permission of the publishers, authors and/or artists.

The cover picture of Apollo is from a painted interior of a white ceramic kylix found at Delphi and dated at circa 470 B.C. The figure represents Apollo, Greek God of Music, Healing, and the Sun, in a ritual act of pouring a libation.

Library of Congress Cataloging-in-Publication Data

Beaulieu, John.
    Music & sound in the healing arts.

    Bibliography: p.
    1. Music therapy.   I. Title.   II. Title: Music
and sound in the healing arts.
ML3920.B26   1987   615.8'5154   87-18095
ISBN 0-88268-057-9
ISBN 0-88268-056-0 (pbk.)

Contents

Dedicated to the five people
the five archetypal elements
which have interacted inside me on this journey

My Mother and Father for their unconditional love
Satya Sai Baba for spiritual guidance
Franz Kamin for musical guidance
Dr. Randolph Stone for healing guidance

Preface

Having played piano at an early age, I can remember making up musical stories about rain, lightning, fire, and thunder. When I became aware of household dynamics, I began to understand that certain pieces of music had definite effects on members of my family. I remember playing "Moon River" in a watery style to dispel potential arguments. It wasn't long before I developed a sixth sense for what music to play to influence different household situations.

I accepted the power of music without question during those early years and into my twenties. Without formal training in healing, I experienced how music affected me as well as those around me. Later, in my tours as a musician, I performed many different styles of music (experimental, classical, rock, folk, country, and blues) and met thousands of people. I noticed that the same piece of music played in different ways would bring a different response from audiences. We would play music to make people drink, fight, want sex, have visions, become sad, happy, inspired, spend money, and gain confidence.

Looking back, I see that this kind of musical expression found in my tours was yet another laboratory for music therapy. Later, working as a therapist in hospitals, I was able to apply my musical abilities to help others discover a richer life. However depressed a person was, the correct selection of music would always awaken their feelings. Doctors and nurses attended my groups. In my opinion, many doctors had sacrificed the childlike quality in themselves to justify the seriousness of their work. As a musician it is very important to acknowledge and embrace the child within. In my music groups doctors benefited enormously. Their inner child could at last wake up, remember, and for a moment experience what good musicians never lose. During those moments the beauty and power of music was appreciated by all of us. Even so, these professionals still had trouble connecting music with their own healing work.

Whenever I met with musicians too, there was always an attitude of ambivalence surrounding the topic of music and healing. Everyone wanted to play and compose music that would be accepted and also contribute to other peoples lives. But exactly how that would happen, or how their music could affect people, was never discussed. What right had they, as musicians, to talk about the possibility of changing people physically and emotionally through the sounds they were making.

Nonetheless, I know that music does cause physical and emotional changes in people. I draw this conclusion partly from my childhood intuition and how I affected my family, and partly from my experiences as a therapist. But in the early years of my work, I did not have an adequate language to describe what I was experiencing. To explain music and healing together within the context of a medical model never made sense. It was like trying to put a round peg in a square hole.

I loved music and I loved working with people, but when I worked in the hospitals I was like an enthusiastic child who hadn't learned how to speak. Every time I had to justify myself to the medical establishment I always felt cowed and insecure, like a child. I translated that to mean I would stay a child, and they would be the grown-ups who have to face the effects of disease.

I was in the same quandary as most musicians who do not want to be held responsible for the powerful influence that music can have on healing. And yet as a therapist I had to be accountable for my methods. Medicine, as much as it can be criticized, strives for accountability.

It was at this time during these early music groups in the medical institutions that I first decided to take responsibility to integrate the child and the grown-up, the musician and the therapist, in order to understand and better communicate the effects of music. In terms of the body I became a naturopathic physician. As part of my training I studied shiatsu, acupuncture, Polarity Therapy, and Ayruveda, the traditional healing of India. I also studied traditional counseling as well as humanistic and transpersonal approaches to psychotherapy.

The ancient physicians and musicians were well aware of the healing properties of music and sound. It was a method for spiritual growth and healing the emotions and body. Once I was able to let go of the idea that spirit and body were separate, the writings of these ancient doctors began to make sense. I believe their insights can help create a new model for living today.

This book is based on my seventeen years of experimentation, observation, and experience in assisting people through music and sound. It presents theory and applications to guide anyone interested in understanding and using music as a powerful means of healing, for themselves and others.

There are many people who have contributed to and supported this book. I prefer to think of it as a group process. I have had the honor of leading the group. I wish to thank all my students for pressing me for clearer and clearer explanations and holding me to the truth. I wish to thank my partner Howard Moskow for his years of support and encouragement. I thank the founders of The Sound School: David Gonzalez, Lisa Sokalov, Frank Bosco, Judy Rubin, and Louise Montello for their professional dedication to an energetic approach to music healing which has inspired me to complete this work. My gratitude also to the coordinators of the New York and Boston Polarity Wellness schools, Amrit Vein and Gary Strauss for believing in this book. I thank my friends and colleagues Peter Wydler and Ueli Gasser as well as all the students, staff, and teachers of the Schule fuer Polarity Wellness in Zurich, Switzerland. I thank my friend Peter Wetzler, a composer who understands editing as musical composition. I thank Carol (Tuynman) of Ear Magazine for professional editing with the heart of a musician. I thank Thea Keats for helping shape my heart into the text. I thank Georgio Palminsino for his special photographic touch and Stephanie Tevonian and everyone at Works for drawing, designing, listening and understanding. I thank Charles Stein for a soft nudge with good timing.

There are many people whose friendship has been a constant source of guidance and I send them all a special light for helping to create this text: Katia Dich, Larry Galante, Jonathan Goldman, Pamela Beaulieu, Nanci Beaulieu, Tom Boni, Stephie Yost, Elisabeth Macrae, Suzanne and Scott Lawrence, Elizabeth Bram, Susan and Frieda Green, Marcia Tumpowsky, and all those beings beyond my current memory and yet in my consciousness.

I thank my son Lars for understanding and supporting the writing of this text. During the hours, days, weeks, and years of writing, editing, thinking and sometimes being lost in abstractions he was always there. He has influenced me deeply. He is truly the representation of the interval of a fifth in our family.

I thank everyone at Station Hill Press—especially Richard Gummere—for going beyond the expected for this text to become reality.

I thank my friends and publishers George and Susan Quasha for guiding this text into being, like pronouncing a special mantra which only they can whisper as Apollo listens from his new home on the cover they created. The heart moves in mysterious pulsations, something from a long time ago is complete, the heart is healed and the unknown is warmer.

Prelude

The premise of this book is that music affects life energy. Contemplating this premise leads us to important questions.

What is music?

How does music affect us physically, emotionally, mentally, and spiritually?

What is energy?

What is life energy?

What is the relationship between music and life energy?

This text begins with an inquiry into these questions. The attempt to understand these questions has been going on from antiquity to the present.

It is important to note that the proof of these investigations will not simply be based on logical arguments. The proof will be in the actual experience of music as an empirical model of life energy.

If you are the type of reader who wants to begin with experience rather than inquiry, then I suggest you begin with the musical experiences available in the chapters on Voice Energetics, Tuning Forks, Mantra, Toning, and Music. For example, you can tap the tuning forks and be aware of your experience. You can listen to different types of music and observe your "gut-level" reactions.

The experience of music is the germinating seed of this book.

This book is directed towards understanding our musical experiences in the context of a life-energy approach to the healing arts.

Our destination is the accountable application of these experiences for healing and increased well-being for ourselves and others.

Let the journey begin.

EAR

The ear has 3 separate parts, each with different rôles in the mechanism of HEARING:-

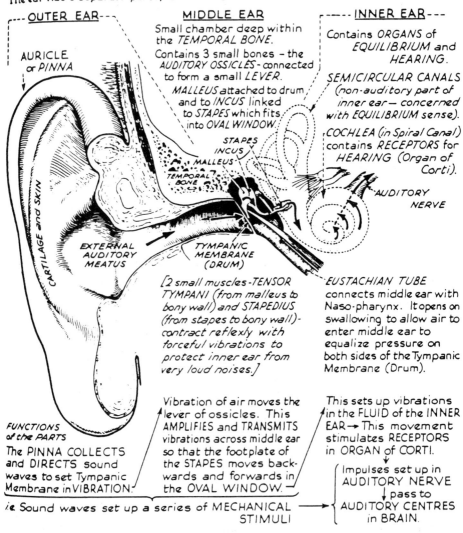

OUTER EAR

AURICLE or PINNA

CARTILAGE and SKIN

EXTERNAL AUDITORY MEATUS

TYMPANIC MEMBRANE (DRUM)

FUNCTIONS of the PARTS

The PINNA COLLECTS and DIRECTS sound waves to set Tympanic Membrane in VIBRATION.

MIDDLE EAR

Small chamber deep within the TEMPORAL BONE.
Contains 3 small bones – the AUDITORY OSSICLES - connected to form a small LEVER.
MALLEUS attached to drum, and to INCUS linked to STAPES which fits into OVAL WINDOW.

STAPES
INCUS
MALLEUS
TEMPORAL BONE

[2 small muscles -TENSOR TYMPANI (from malleus to bony wall) and STAPEDIUS (from stapes to bony wall)- contract reflexly with forceful vibrations to protect inner ear from very loud noises.]

Vibration of air moves the lever of ossicles. This AMPLIFIES and TRANSMITS vibrations across middle ear so that the footplate of the STAPES moves back-wards and forwards in the OVAL WINDOW.

INNER EAR

Contains ORGANS of EQUILIBRIUM and HEARING.
SEMICIRCULAR CANALS (non-auditory part of inner ear — concerned with EQUILIBRIUM sense).
COCHLEA (in Spiral Canal) contains RECEPTORS for HEARING (Organ of Corti).

AUDITORY NERVE

EUSTACHIAN TUBE connects middle ear with Naso-pharynx. It opens on swallowing to allow air to enter middle ear to equalize pressure on both sides of the Tympanic Membrane (Drum).

This sets up vibrations in the FLUID of the INNER EAR → This movement stimulates RECEPTORS in ORGAN of CORTI.

Impulses set up in AUDITORY NERVE pass to AUDITORY CENTRES in BRAIN.

ie Sound waves set up a series of MECHANICAL STIMULI

Listening

What is music? Simply stated, music is the appreciation of sound. All sounds are potentially music. It is unfortunate that for many people music is limited to concert halls, specific composers, styles of music, or certain predetermined musical instruments. I enjoy listening to the music of birds, waves, horns, and people talking. I also enjoy listening to Bach, Mozart, the Beatles and John Cage.

The way we appreciate sounds is through listening. When sounds are listened to—and not merely "heard"—they become music. This is why the act of listening is an art. It begins with hearing but goes much deeper. There are several different approaches to understanding the art of listening. For example in the Hindu tradition listening is divided into four levels, or *koshas* (sheaths). The first is the level of meaning. The second is the level of feeling, or subtle form. The third is an intense and constant awareness or presence, and the fourth level is known as the "soundless sound."

I have divided listening into five levels. These are called Hearing, Imagination, Realities, Elements, and Silence. Each level can be directly experienced. These levels are my mappings. They are references for relating common experiences within the vastness of sound.

I. Hearing. Listening begins with hearing. All sounds that we hear with our ears are available for listening. This includes train whistles, speech, horns, musical pitches, vacuum cleaners, all music, cars, etc. It is important to note that there is no such thing as a "good" or a "bad" sound; these value judgments interfere with our perception and enjoyment of the deeper aspects of sound. I remember as a child beating on a tin can and enjoying the different rhythms. The man next door said, "Stop that noise!" I was listening and he was hearing. When we hear something and do not allow ourselves to listen it becomes noise.

II. Imagination. All sounds have the potential to rouse our imagination. When entering this level of sound make sure you are physically safe.

Once, while teaching a class out-of-doors at Kingsborough College in Brooklyn I heard a very deep-low sound. I could not figure out where it was coming from. It kept getting louder and louder until even the buildings were vibrating with the sound. The sound seemed everywhere; I could feel my body shake. I stopped teaching my class (it was useless to try talking over the sound) and ran to the nearby ocean, sat down, and surrendered to the sound. I had never heard anything like it. I was having visions. I thought the Apocalypse was coming. It seemed like the sound would go on forever, and I definitely prepared myself to leave with it. However, as it turned out, the sound passed and I walked back to my students. They had continued talking the whole time as if they hadn't heard the sound. I was somewhat shocked by their behavior, as I am sure they were by mine. Then one of the students looked at me a little puzzled and said, "John, it was only the Concord SST taking off from Kennedy airport."

I had let my imagination go with the sound, while my students had just identified the sound "as a Concord" and left it at that. The level of imagination is giving ourselves permission to have images with the sounds. For example, when we go to a concert we do not simply "hear violins"; we close our eyes and let the music take us to magical places.

III. Realities. Music has the power to bypass our conscious focus of attention. We can actually become the music. And conversely, we are what we listen to. It is not that difficult to recognize people by the type of music they listen to. People who like punk rock appear different from people who listen to early classical, and people who listen to jazz are different from others who listen to rock 'n' roll.

When I was in music school there were certain people who only liked to listen to J. S. Bach. They were Bach fanatics. As far as they were concerned Bach was all there was in music. There were other people who listened only to Beethoven. I would sit with my friends in the student lounge and we would pick out the Beethovens from the Bachs. The Bachs always walked fast with a bounce. The Beethovens walked slower and more straight forward. They always looked very serious.

In his book, *Music, Its Secret Influence Throughout the Ages,* Cyril Scott relates the evolution of whole cultures to their listening tastes:

> . . . wherever the greatest variety of music
> styles has been obtained, there the adherence to tra-
> dition and custom has been proportionately less
> marked; and where musical styles are limited, as
> for instance, in China, adherence to—nay, even

worship of—tradition obtains to a marked degree.
We are fully aware that on stating this we would
seem to be lending weight to the prevalent notion
that styles of music are merely the outcome and
expression of civilizations and national feelings —
that is to say that the civilization comes first, and its
characteristic species of music afterwards. But an
examination of history proves the truth to be exactly
the reverse: an innovation in musical style has
invariably been followed by an innovation in poli-
tics and morals. [1]

During the summer of 1984 I visited an isolated "hippie commune" near Big Sur, California. I thought I was back in 1965. After two days I realized that the only music being played was early Jefferson Airplane, Grateful Dead, Buffalo Springfield, etc. Everyone still wore long hair and expressed hippie values. I discovered that as a group they selected the music that was to be allowed in the commune. This music obviously helped them to sustain—or even determine—their reality. I wondered: Would their reality change if their music changed?

When the Ayatollah Khomeini became the leader of Iran one of his first acts was to outlaw all forms of music other than traditional Iranian. What would happen to American reality if we passed laws that people could only listen to early country and western?

The key to conscious listening is flexibility. Through listening, we have the ability to seek out and enter sound. When we freely resonate with sound(s) we enter into and become the sound. We are viewing the world through the sound and learn that sounds do not explain themselves; sounds reveal themselves. There are as many revelations as there are sounds and combinations of sounds, but we have to be flexible and free to move through the various realities that sounds create.

For example, I was walking down a New York street with two friends. The trucks were idling, and the workers were unloading crates. Something about the sound of the trucks caught my attention. I asked my friends if they would be willing to watch out for my safety while I sat down and listened more deeply to the sound of the trucks.

I sat in a safe spot and allowed my body and mind to relax. The sounds of the trucks formed a distinct rhythm: da-da-daa—boom, da-da da-da-daa—boom, etc. I let myself go with the sound. At first I imagined being a teenager in Indiana and going to the drag races and listening to the sound of the engines idle. I remembered how these sounds fascinated me, and I imagined driving a race car.

Listening even deeper to the sound I felt myself "move inside" its pulse. My imagination and memories were still present, now accompanied by a new sensation. A profound quietness or stillness came and, for a moment, I experienced myself just being the sound.

Then there was a shift in my awareness, and I found myself with a group of Aborigine chanters. They were communicating a message about "dream time." I was just as clearly with them as I had been with the truck just a few minutes ago. I allowed myself to absorb their message. An old man signaled that they must move on into the desert. I understood.

At that moment a friend tapped me on the shoulder, I came back to the reality of a New York City street. The truck was driving away.

IV. Elements. "Element listening" is the primary focus of this text. To begin understanding this level, imagine different environments. For example, Alaska is cold and windy. The Sahara desert is hot and dry. The rain forests of the Amazon are hot, humid, and wet. The natural elements in these environments mix in different ways to create realities within which people live. Their customs, dress, thoughts, and physical appearances can all be understood in relationship to the elements.

Music also creates environments. Element listening is looking through the reality around a music to the elements that give rise to that reality. If there are no barriers to internal perception, then the physical body will respond like the sounding board of a piano. It will resonate with the qualities of the sound. The mind, if it is not involved with judging the sensations, will be free to observe the effects. The descriptions usually emerge as a felt sense which is expressed in a gut-level primitive language. For example: I just wanted to jump up and down. I wanted to sit. I felt like running. Sometimes words associated with nature will spontaneously come from the felt sense. For example: I felt it flowing like water. I felt like a fire out of control.

In the past, the "gut-level" feelings of music were associated with human behavior and the qualities of natural elements. These primal feelings were given the labels Ether (silence), Air, Fire, Water, and Earth. Due to our great advances in technology, it is easy to be out of touch with the validity of our basic feeling responses. We tend to trust a machine more than ourselves. Listening on an elemental level requires a trust in our own primitive perceptions. Combined with a life-energy model of healing, these perceptions become important information.

V. Silence. The deepest level of listening is silence. The center of all sound is silence. All sounds rise from and lead back to silence. Listening is the art of discovering silence. Silence is the key to the many adventures the world of sound has to offer. Through silence we are truly safe and free. We know the beginning and we know the end.

(Silence)

Life Energy

Energy

It was not until the twentieth century that physicists discovered that mass and energy were interchangeable. This relationship was defined by Einstein in 1905 in the equation $E=mc^2$ where energy is equal to mass times the speed of light squared. The power of Einstein's formulation is clearly demonstrated in nuclear weapons. For example, the amount of mass converted into energy in the destruction of Hiroshima was about one-thirtieth of an ounce. It would have required twelve thousand five hundred tons of TNT to release the same amount of energy. An even more graphic comparison is described by Jonathan Schell in his book *The Fate of the Earth:* "The energy yielded by application of the universal physics of the twentieth century exceeds the energy yielded by the terrestrial, or planetary, physics of the nineteenth century as the cosmos exceeds the earth."[1]

It is unfortunate that scientific proof of the unification of matter and energy had to find its first expression in an act of war. However, nuclear weapons, as uncomfortable as they make us, do have a positive aspect. They are constant reminders that everything we know, including ourselves, can at any moment be converted to energy! The flashes of light at Hiroshima, Nagasaki, and Bikini Atoll were like cosmic alarm clocks telling us to wake up.

We had been like birds in a shell until the twentieth century broke in upon us. We had been protected and isolated from the power of the universe. Now we are embarking upon a new journey. The safety of our earthly shell is crumbling. A higher order of being must emerge. The time has come for us to enter into a unified journey. Like a bird leaving its shell, we must coordinate all the parts of ourselves into a magnificent flying organism.

Life Energy

I believe understanding energy in the healing arts will play a central role in our transition into beings of higher states of energy. The following chart developed by the late Dr. Randolph Stone is a composite picture of us as energy beings.

Dr. Stone understood "New Energy Physics" in terms of ourselves. He taught that our bodies are not solid, but are a coordinated pattern of energy movement. The lines in the chart represent the ideal pattern of energy, and should be visualized as swirling movement. Sickness results when the flow of energy is inhibited or disrupted. He called his method of restoring energy flow Polarity Therapy.

COMPOSITE PICTURE OF THE PATTERN FORCES
OF THE BODY AND THEIR WIRELESS CIRCUITS.

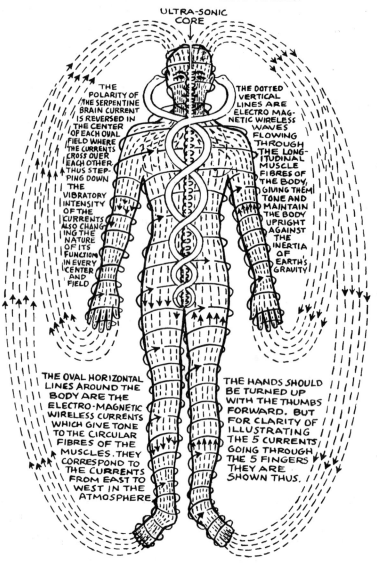

ULTRA-SONIC CORE

THE POLARITY OF THE SERPENTINE BRAIN CURRENT IS REVERSED IN THE CENTER OF EACH OVAL FIELD WHERE THE CURRENTS CROSS OVER EACH OTHER. THUS STEPPING DOWN THE VIBRATORY INTENSITY OF THE CURRENTS ALSO CHANGING THE NATURE OF ITS FUNCTION IN EVERY CENTER AND FIELD

THE DOTTED VERTICAL LINES ARE ELECTRO MAGNETIC WIRELESS WAVES FLOWING THROUGH THE LONGITUDINAL MUSCLE FIBRES OF THE BODY, GIVING THEM TONE AND MAINTAIN THE BODY UPRIGHT AGAINST THE INERTIA OF EARTH'S GRAVITY

THE OVAL HORIZONTAL LINES AROUND THE BODY ARE THE ELECTRO-MAGNETIC WIRELESS CURRENTS WHICH GIVE TONE TO THE CIRCULAR FIBRES OF THE MUSCLES. THEY CORRESPOND TO THE CURRENTS FROM EAST TO WEST IN THE ATMOSPHERE.

THE HANDS SHOULD BE TURNED UP WITH THE THUMBS FORWARD. BUT FOR CLARITY OF ILLUSTRATING THE 5 CURRENTS GOING THROUGH THE 5 FINGERS THEY ARE SHOWN THUS.

Other teachers and cultures have presented similar models for understanding life energy. Hippocrates called it *vis medicatrix naturae* (the healing power of nature). Life energy was known to the Chinese as Chi and is the basis for the acupuncture system of healing. In India, life energy is known as Prana and is the foundation of Ayruveda, the natural healing practices of India. The late Dr. Wilhelm Reich referred to life energy as orgone energy. He developed a system of psychotherapy based on increasing energy. Reich referred to the movement of life energy as "streaming" and the coordinated movement of a whole energy field as "oceanic." In his text *Cosmic Superimposition* he attempted to show the relationship between life energy, sexuality, movements of the oceans, and star systems. Wilhelm Reich died in prison because he challenged the foundations of traditional medicine. I believe his story represents an ingrained cultural fear about perceiving ourselves as beings of energy.

The roots of this fear relate back to the seventeenth century and the philosopher René Descartes. In his text *Traité de L'Homme*, Descartes saw the universe as being divided into two separate parts. One division was that of mind or spirit, which he termed *res cogitans*, and the other was matter, or *res extensas*. Within his model, the physical body was seen as a machine and a doctor's training revolved around maintaining and fixing up the "body-machine." The soul, mind, and life force were separate from the body machine. They were under the authority of the Church and not to be tampered with by medicine.

The penalty for a doctor infringing upon the realm of the church could mean death or imprisonment. This was the fate of Wilhelm Reich as late as 1956. Since music is considered by the church to be an expression of the soul, it is not surprising that to this day doctors pay little attention to its healing properties.

In the latter part of the seventeenth century Sir Isaac Newton validated Descartes' philosophy. He pioneered a physics based upon the principle that mass and energy constitute two separate closed systems. His belief was expressed in the conservation laws of nineteenth-century physics: the law of the conservation of energy and the law of the conservation of mass. Therefore even when the Church began to lose power, the scientific investigations of the eighteenth and nineteenth centuries continued to validate a separate universe.

In contrast to the philosophy of separateness, the primary role of energy in the healing arts comes from a holistic philosophy. Holism assumes that each individual is unique and represents a complex interaction of body, emotion, mind, and spirit. Health exists when these elements function in harmony with themselves as well as with the cosmos. Disorders or disease become evident when parts of the whole are experienced as separate and conflicting. This viewpoint is further supported by the investigations of modern physicists. Dr. Fritjof Capra reflects the current scientific viewpoint in these words: "The universe is no longer seen as a machine made up of a multitude of objects, but rather as a harmonious 'organic' whole whose parts are only defined through their interrelations."[2]

Wellness

Today, the relationship of life energy to traditional medicine is best summarized in the following Wellness Continuum developed by Dr. John Travis:

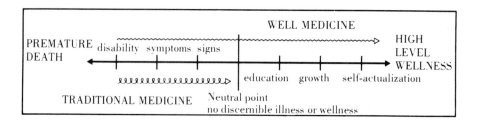

Moving from the center to the left shows a progressively worsening state of health—decreasing energy. Moving to the right of center shows increasing levels of health and well-being—increasing energy. Traditional medicine is oriented towards curing evidence of disease, but usually stops at the midpoint. Well medicine begins at any point of the scale with the goal of helping a person move as far to the right as he is willing to go.[3]

Wellness is always expanding and growing. According to Travis, "Wellness is an efficient channeling of energy—energy received from the environment, transformed within you, and sent on to affect the world outside."[4] The more efficient the channeling of life energy the more

healthy one will be. There is no end point to the level of energy obtaina-
ble.

The journey into higher levels of wellness-energy begins anywhere on
the continuum by taking responsibility for how we utilize life energy. A
choice is made to learn and practice the art of moving to the right on the
continuum. Wherever we are in time we choose those lifestyle practices
which support and assist us in achieving our highest state of well-being.
Wellness is our responsibility. Everything we do—spiritually, mentally,
emotionally, and physically—has an effect upon our health.

Elements:
The Language of Energy

The principles of energy movement are based upon the division of energy into the five elements: Ether, Air, Fire, Water, and Earth. On a cosmic scale, each element symbolizes a universal principle or archetype. Each element is transcendental. These elements combine and interact to create and motivate all life.

The existence of archetypal elements is recognized in the philosophical, religious, and healing traditions of many cultures. All speak of one primary energy, which they often refer to as sound, that then divides and steps down in currents of element energy. Dr. Vasant Lad describes this process of division from an Ayruvedic perspective:

> The rishies perceived that in the beginning the world existed in an unmanifested state of consciousness. From that state of unified consciousness, the subtle vibrations of the cosmic soundless sound aum manifested. From that vibration there first appeared the Ether element. This ethereal element then began to move: its subtle movements created the Air, which is Ether in action. The movement of Ether produced friction, and through that friction heat was generated. Particles of heat-energy combined to form intense light and from this light the Fire element manifested.
>
> Thus, Ether manifested into Air, and it was the same Ether that further manifested into Fire. Through the heat of the Fire, certain ethereal elements dissolved and liquified, manifesting the Water element, and then solidified to form the molecules of Earth. In this way, Ether manifested into the four elements of Air, Fire, Water, and Earth.[1]

Chinese philosophy and healing are also based upon the concept of the five elements. The elements Wood, Fire, Earth, Metal, and Water encompass all natural phenomena. This symbolism applies itself equally to man. Although the names of the Chinese elements are different, the underlying principles are universal.

The elements were also known in the Western traditions. Greek philosophy was based on a doctrine of the elements. Man's four faculties: moral (Fire), aesthetic and soul (Water), intellectual (Air), and physical (Earth) were seen as expressions of the elements. Hippocrates, the father of Western medicine, based his healing on the four moods, or humours. He termed them phlegmatic (Earth), choleric (Water), sanguine (Fire), and melancholic (Air). The elements were rediscovered in the Middle Ages and Renaissance, most interestingly by three distinguished scholars concerned with the "music of the spheres": the Jesuit Father Athansasius Kircher, the English Rosicrucian Robert Fludd, and the astronomer Johannes Kepler. Robert Fludd's World Monochord illustrates the relationship of the elements to sound and creation.

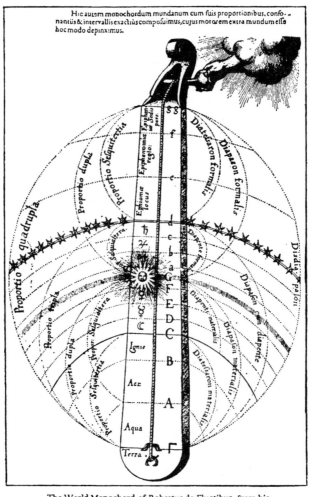

The World-Monochord of Robertus de Fluctibus, from his
Metaphysica, physica atque technica ... Historia, Linz 1519.

Fritz Stege explains the World Monochord in *Music, Magic, Mystery*.

> The single-stringed measuring instrument with
> whose aid Pythagoreans worked out the intervals is
> anchored to Earth (Terra). The latter corresponds
> to the Gamma Graecum, the bottom note of the
> medieval note-system. Above it lie at intervals of a
> second the other elements Aqua, Aer, Ignis
> (Water, Air, Fire) and thus in fact the whole mate-
> rial world.[2]

The following chart shows ourselves in relationship to the elements.

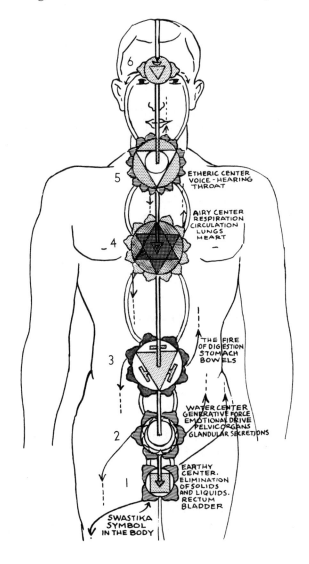

6

5   ETHERIC CENTER
VOICE - HEARING
THROAT

AIRY CENTER
RESPIRATION
CIRCULATION
LUNGS
HEART

4

THE FIRE
OF DIGESTION
STOMACH
BOWELS

3

WATER CENTER
GENERATIVE FORCE
EMOTIONAL DRIVE
PELVIC ORGANS
GLANDULAR SECRETIONS

2

EARTHY
CENTER.
ELIMINATION
OF SOLIDS
AND LIQUIDS.
RECTUM
BLADDER

1

SWASTIKA
SYMBOL
IN THE BODY

At the center of the chart are three primary energy currents. These are illustrated as the ultrasonic core in the middle, with two intertwined lines. Together they form the symbol of the caduceus. The caduceus, or the Staff of Hermes, was the insignia of the ancient physicians of Egypt and Greece.

Dr. Stone explains the meaning of the caduceus symbol:

> The two serpents represent the Mind Principle in its dual aspect. The fiery breath of the Sun is the positive pole as the vital energy on the right side of the body. It was called "Yang" by the Chinese, and "Pingala" by the Hindus. On the left side of the body flows the cooling energy of the Moon essence of Nature. This was called "Yin" by the Chinese, and the "Ida" current in India.[3]

Although the caduceus remains the physicians' symbol, its true energy meaning is not recognized by those practicing medicine today.

The currents of the caduceus can be visualized as a wave energy that divides to create element centers or chakras. The term chakra comes from Sanskrit and means "spinning wheel of energy." The chakras are symbolized in the diagram by lotus flowers with decreasing numbers of petals depicting a step down in vibration. In ancient drawings the chakras were pictured as spinning wheels without symbolic embellishment.

In terms of life energy, the polarities of + (positive) and - (negative) are represented by the two snakes of the caduceus. The ultrasonic core is neutral. At each chakra, the two snakes create Air polarities, Fire polarities, Water polarities, and Earth polarities. A measure of wellness is flexibility, the individual's ability to move with the elements. Illness is a suppression of element expression.

For example, let us say a man is in a situation where he is required to make quick movements (+ Air) and be loud (+ Fire). Two hours later the situation changes, requiring him to slow down (+ Earth) and talk with a flowing voice (+ Water). When this man cannot make the element transition from + Air and Fire to + Water and Earth, he is not in harmony with the requirements of the environment. If he can be flexible with the elements, the transition will take place automatically.

There is no set formula for balancing the elements in a person. It is a mobile, ever-changing interaction of elements between the self, the external environment, and the cosmos. There is only an individual's ability to participate with each element at the appropriate time.

Illness takes place when element flexibility is lost. Stress is defined as a pressure or strain requiring change. When we are unable to adapt to such unbalancing forces and change, stress becomes distress. When we are flexible enough to change, stress becomes euphoria.

When an element transition does not take place, the elements seeking natural expression are held or suppressed. This process begins in the mind. The mind is the conductor of the elements. Dr. Stone states, "Mind, being a neutral activity in itself, is therefore capable of every capacity of action and sensation through matter." However, if the mind takes on a charge, then it loses its neutrality and the result is the suppression of an element or elements.

The elements are not good or bad. Nature has no morals or ethics. The mind creates morals and ethics that may or may not be in alignment with the movements of nature. These morals lead to judgments and restriction of behavior. For example, an individual will not raise his voice because he judges loudness as "bad." He reasons that his father is loud and he is not going to be like his father. On an elemental level, he judged the Fire as bad, and therefore consciously and unconsciously held back any Fiery expression. Externally he remains polite and quiet. He will not get loud under any circumstances.

When the elements are suppressed, they will seek other forms of expression that may be unproductive to the individual. In the above instance, the Fire eventually sought expression through the physical body in the form of an ulcer. The ulcer irritated the man so much that he said he "wanted to scream."

This man's case shows how important it is to understand the qualities of each element. The following paragraphs are examples of each element and their special characteristics.

Ether

Ether is space. Musically it is the space of the diapason, or octave, where all tones exist. It is like a vessel that contains everything.

The ancient alchemists referred to Ether as the quintessence. It was considered to be the highest element, the mixing bowl in which the other four lower elements were formed. Ether relates directly to sound and is associated with hearing. If we can go to a place where there is a deep silence, and close our eyes and listen, eventually we can become aware of something behind the silence . . . a noiseless sound. This is the element Ether.

> At the etheric level only one sense exists, but at the
> earth level there are five senses. At the etheric
> level we can only hear; air, however, can be heard
> and felt; fire can be heard, felt and seen; water can
> be heard, felt, seen and tasted; and finally earth
> can be cognized by all five senses.[4]

Ether represents open-spatial movement. The space between the joints and the free movement of the bones of the cranium require the presence of Ether. The focal point of Ether is in the throat. The voice can take on the quality of any of the four lower elements. This is discussed in depth in the chapter on Voice Energetics.

Air

The next step down of energy creates the element Air. This element is represented by the heart chakra. Air, the least tangible of the four elements, is everywhere — volatile, breezy, shifting, clear, and transparent. Air represents the mind and intellect. A person exhibiting the Air quality has hundreds of ideas and tends to be philosophical and rational about their emotions. When we say that someone is "in their head," or is "all over the place," we are noticing the presence of the element Air.

On the physical level, Air is manifested as movement and in the act of touching. In the words of Dr. Stone, "the Air element moves zigzag, like lightning or the motion of a worm, or the small intestines in action." Airy movement is light, expansive, buoyant, fast, and shaky. When someone says, "I can't seem to hold still," or they are always "on the move," we can then again assume the presence of Air.

Bodily Air creates respiration and is associated with the lungs, heart, and circulation. The blood passes through the heart and lungs and carries the movement of oxygen to every cell in the body. Without this continuous movement or circulation we would die. Air also manifests as gas in the body. Gaseous swelling is an example of an excess of Air in the intestines.

Fire

The ten-petaled lotus flower in the center of the diaphragm represents the Fire element. Fire cannot be contained in one shape, one size, or one form. Dr. Stone says, "The Fire element flies upward like sparks in the hearth." Fire represents the quality of vision; bringing light into darkness.

Fire can be expressed in terms of fantasy. Someone with a lot of Fire would tend to fantasize, dramatize, and think towards the future. On an emotional level the person with Fire is "burning" with enthusiasm. Fire also has in it the possibility of becoming volatile, of being out of control. It can consume everything. When the Fire is suppressed, it may look like there is a lack of motivation or an inability to take action.

Physically, Fire is seen in running, staccato, leaping, driving movement. Whereas Air is zigzag and all over the place, Fire has a definite direction. The sayings "let's go get them" or "full steam ahead" suggest Fire.

The organs of digestion, stomach, and bowels are directly related to Fire. Too much or too little Fire leads to poor digestion. Fire also relates to metabolism and body-heat regulation. A fever is Fire rising in the body. Fever burns away unnecessary Earth, Water, and Air. The place of Fire in the body is in the head, eyes, and nervous system.

Water

The element Water is symbolized by the six-petaled lotus located just below the navel. Water is experienced as fluidity. Its movement flows down.

On the mental level, Water manifests itself in the form of creativity. It represents the organs of reproductivity and the creation of new life. On an emotional level, Water is associated with attachment and deep feelings. Possessiveness and jealousy are examples of the attachments of Water.

On the physical level, Water is associated with the generative force and glandular secretions necessary for sexuality. Water in the blood lubricates the entire body. We cannot live without it.

Earth

We stand on earth, build on earth, and grow food in the earth. Earth is real, solid, reliable, and factual. On the mental level, the Earth element is characterized by a person's readiness to be organized and efficient. "It's just good ole common sense" represents an Earthy statement.

Earth serves as the foundation for the other elements. The saying "having one's feet on the ground" implies Earth's providing a solid base of support. Emotionally, this is reflected in a sense of security. When Earth is not present there is fear and insecurity. A person with little Earth will often compensate by becoming rigid or stiff. On the mental level this may appear as someone being very dogmatic or opinionated.

On the physical level, Earth is associated with the skeletal system and the elimination of solid waste. Earth movement is slow, verging on stillness. In contrast to Air, Earth is never in a hurry. It takes its time, like walking through the cornfields of Indiana on a hot summer day.

Case Studies

I have been practicing energy-based healing for seventeen years. At the most I feel as though I am a "qualified beginner." During my travels in India I met an Ayruvedic physician. He was eighty years old and it was his seventy-first year of practicing energy healing. He was born into a family of physicians and began studying when he was nine years old. He was a very humble man. During my visit he chanted the Vedas and looked into my eyes. At that moment I realized the depths of energy healing. Later he explained to me that he had much more to learn.

I suggest you approach the following studies keeping the above story in mind.

Case A. The individual spoke of future plans and goals in an excited way (Fire with Air). She believed her life would change (Fire). At the same time she had trouble when it came to paying for her session (Earth). When asked her reason for having a session her reply was, "just to slow down some." There were no strong physical complaints.

Evaluation. She has + Fire with + Air and - Water with - Earth. This elemental pattern is mental and has not manifested strongly in the physical body, although some signs are appearing: slight premenstrual syndrome (PMS) with brief lower backaches and general nervousness reflected in not being able to slow down. PMS is associated with the suppression of the Water element. Not being able to slow down is a suppression of the Earth element. Sometimes she just runs out of energy and goes into a slump. This means that she burns up Fire and Air and literally slumps into the heavier elements of Earth and Water.

Recommendations. She was asked to listen to Brahms. (Please note: The methods for making musical recommendations and voice evaluations are explained in depth in the chapters on Music and Voice Energetics.) She was also given a Ether-Water-Earth mantra with instructions on how to sit with it for ten minutes a day. During counseling she was instructed to speak slower and to connect her words. When she did this, she began to cry (suppressed Water surfacing). She was asked to outline her steps for reaching future goals (Earth).

After several sessions she got in touch with the qualities of Earth and Water in her life. She realized the mental barriers to their expression and opened herself up to the feelings of these elements in her body. If the pattern of suppressing these elements had continued, it could have taken the physical form of fibroids, ovarian cysts, or tumors (suppressed Earth) located in the pelvic region (Water).

Case B. A man was jittery and not able to sleep. He talked very fast and switched topics (+ Air). After eating he would become bloated and later pass gas (+ Air). His life was overstructured (+ Earth). His digestion was slow (- Fire) and he tended towards constipation.

Evaluation. Air is trapped within Earth. The Air shows up as gas or "jittery behavior." Fire is negative and suppressed in the colon. Constipation results, evaporating the Water and causing the Earth element to form hard walls.

Recommendations. He was asked to listen to slow jazz to soften the Earth walls and quiet the Fire, giving the Air freer expression. He was put on a raw foods diet (Water and Earth). He was also given slow-flowing bodywork (Water and Earth) with fast rocking at times (breaking loose Air).

Case C. A woman was twenty-five pounds over her "normal weight." Her extra pounds appeared "watery." She complained of feeling heavy, which she called her depression (Water is heavy and flows downward). She felt frustrated because her children were of age to leave home and she had to face problems with her husband. Her weight began to increase when they found themselves spending more time together. She was unable to assert herself in a fiery way to her husband.

Her Fire was negative and suppressed. Her Water was positive and held. She was stuck on a "titter-totter" between Fire and Water.

Recommendations. She was taught to speak in a supportive Fiery way to her husband. As she learned how to "feel" and express Fire in all areas of her life her weight decreased and she felt light and powerful. When Fire was permitted to surface, the heat boiled the excess Water turning it into steam (hot, moist, rising Air). The steam was utilized as motivation She became so involved with life that her metabolism (Fire) increased. The held Water released and became a source of creative inspiration. Instead of creating children (Water-generation) she began painting (visual Fire with Water).

Music & Life Energy

Instead of using the word "energy" the ancients used the concept of Sacred Sound. Although the words for Sacred Sound changed from culture to culture, the basic meaning remained the same. In Christianity, Sacred Sound is referred to in the Bible as the Word. "In the beginning was the Word, and the Word was with God, and the Word was God." (John 1:1)

Sacred Sound was known in ancient China as "Kung," or the cosmic tone. Some other names for Sacred Sound are soundless sound, the key note, the cosmic sound, and OM. The Sufi Hazrat Inayat Khan expresses Sacred Sound simply and poetically as the word Music:

> Music, the word we use in our everyday language,
> is nothing less than the picture of our Beloved. It is
> because music is the picture of our Beloved that we
> love music. But the question is, what is our
> Beloved and where is our Beloved? Our Beloved is
> that which is our source and our goal; and what we
> see of our Beloved before our physical eyes is the
> beauty which is before us; and that part of our
> Beloved so manifest to our eyes (sacred sound) is
> the inner form of beauty of which our Beloved
> speaks to us. If only we would listen to the voice of
> all the beauty that attracts us in any form, we would
> find that in every aspect it tells us that behind all
> manifestation is the perfect Spirit, the Spirit of wisdom. [1]

Pythagoras of Samos, a Greek mathematician, philosopher, and musician, conceived of the universe as a vast musical instrument. He called the Sacred Sound of the universe "music of the spheres." The ancient rishies, or seers, of India referred to Sacred Sound as Shabda.

> In India, it is said, the universe hangs on sound.
> Not ordinary sound, but a cosmic vibration so mas-
> sive and subtle and all-encompassing that every-
> thing seen and unseen (including man) is filled with it. [2]

It was Pythagoras' view that sound was the link between the gods and man. Discovering Sacred Sound within ourselves is the basis for mantric yoga, Pythagorean intervals, Western classical and modern music, the Indian ragas, Buddhist chanting, the sacred rhythms of African tribes, the trance dance music of Bali as well as many other systems of music and sound.

Audible sound, or simply the sound we hear with our ears, is the gateway to Sacred Sound. It is composed of three characteristics; Wave, Pulse, and Form. These terms have their origin in musical vocabulary and have a new and expanded meaning in the context of life energy. Gurdjieff refers to the relationship of Wave, Pulse, and Form as the "fundamental law" that creates all phenomena:

> This is the "Law of Three" or the law of the three
> principles or the three forces. It consists of the fact
> that every phenomena, on whatever scale and in
> whatever world it may take place, from molecular
> to cosmic phenomena, is the result of the combina-
> tion of the meeting of three different forces. [3]

In Christianity, these organizing principles were known as the trinity: The Father, Son, and Holy Ghost. The Father represents Pulse on a cosmic scale, the Holy Ghost represents Wave, and the Son represents Form. In Hinduism, this is the basis of the underlying trinity of their religion: Brahma, Vishnu, and Shiva. The organizing principle of three is also expressed in the three pillars of the Cabala. The central pillar is Pulse and the two outer pillars represent Form and Wave.

When hearing a sound these qualities are always present. Although they can be talked about separately, they always occur simultaneously. The term pulse is used to describe the generating aspect of sound. Pulse can be simply thought of as the force of expansion and contraction. In musical terms pulse is the same as beat. Without a pulse we would not exist. Dr. Stone referred to the pulse of Sacred Sound within ourselves as the ultrasonic core.

Wave and form are simultaneously created from pulse. They are symbolized in energy language by the two snakes of the caduceus. Usually we think of sound as a Wave. A sound wave is represented in the diagram at the top of the next page.

The rising and falling of the wave shown by the arrows is in alignment with the expansion and contraction of pulse. The original pulse is always contained in the wave. In this diagram, one pulse is equivalent to one complete cycle of the wave. Sound waves are measured in cycles per second (cps). It would also be correct to say pulses per second. Audible sound begins with sixteen cycles (pulses) per second. This is perceived

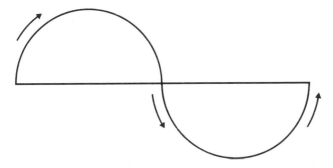

by the ear as a very low-pitched sound. The upper limit of audible sound is approximately eighteen thousand to twenty thousand cycles (pulses) per second.

Form is the more elusive component of sound. Sound-forms can be seen by subjecting mediums such as sand, water, or clay to a continuous sound vibration. The following pictures taken by Dr. Hans Jenny are sound-forms. They were obtained by placing various mediums on a steel plate with a crystal sound oscillator attached to the bottom. The sound

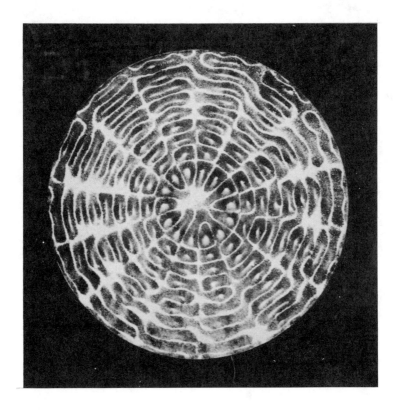

oscillator creates a pulse which vibrates the steel plate. *The forms on the plate are examples of sound organizing matter.* When looking at these pictures remember that the patterns are in constant motion. These pictures are known as Chalinadi figures and are an important part of cymatics, the study of Wave phenomena.

Concerning these pictures Dr. Jenny states:

> Since the various aspects of these phenomena are due to vibration, we are confronted with a spectrum which reveals a patterned, figurative formation at one pole (form) and kinetic-dynamic processes at the other (wave), the whole being generated and

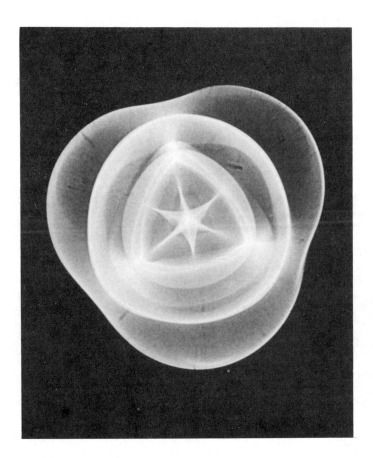

sustained by its essential periodicity. . . . The three
fields—the periodic (pulse) as the fundamental
field with the two poles of figure (form) and dynamic
(wave)—invariably appear as one. They are incon-
ceivable without each other. It is quite out of the
question to take away the one or the other; nothing
can be abstracted without the whole ceasing to
exist. We cannot therefore number them one, two,
three, but can only say they are threefold in appear-
ance and yet unitary; that they appear as one and
yet are threefold.[4]

Other physicists have discovered similar phenomena working with
light and sub-atomic particles.

This property of matter and of light is very strange.
It seems impossible to accept that something can
be at the same time a particle—i.e., an entity

confined to a very small volume of space (form)—
and a wave, which is spread out over a large region
of space. . . . [5]

There is a similarity between cymatics pictures and quantum particles. In both cases that which appears to be a solid form is also a wave.
They are both being created and simultaneously organized by the principle of pulse. This is the great mystery of sound: there is no solidity! A
form that appears solid is actually created by an underlying vibration.

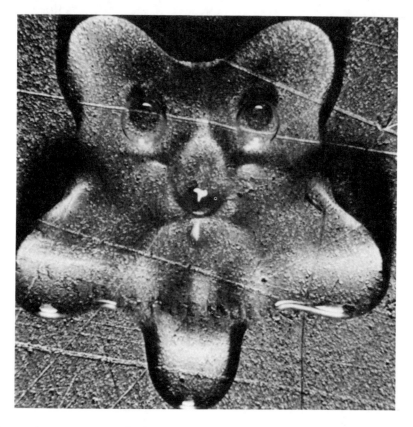

The ancients conceived of our universe as being organized in a manner
similar to that shown in cymatic pictures. For them, everything was a
manifestation of the underlying vibration of Sacred Sound.

To explain the concept of Wave and Form as being one, or the same,
physicists further developed the theory of a quantum field or, in terms of
sound, a fundamental pulse.

The quantum field is seen as the fundamental physical entity: a continuous medium which is present everywhere in space. Particles (forms) are merely local condensations of the field (pulse); concentrations of energy which come and go, thereby losing their individual character and dissolving into the underlying field.

In the words of Albert Einstein: "We may therefore regard matter as being constituted by the regions of Space in which the field is extremely intense.... There is no place in this new kind of physics both for the field and matter, for the field is the only reality."[6]

We are like the vibrating mediums in the cymatics photographs. We too are made up of Pulse, Wave, and Form. However, our conscious awareness seems to identify more with the element of Form, especially when it comes to our physical body. In the West this leads us to place a greater emphasis on materialism, or the knowing of Form. In the East we see a great emphasis on intuition, or the knowing of Wave phenomenon. The widespread introduction of Eastern meditative practices in the West and recent discoveries in physics have made our intuitive qualities more acceptable. All of us are somewhat familiar with this aspect of ourselves. The following story illustrates the differences between the materialistic knowing of the West (Form) and the intuitive knowing of the East (Wave).

During the summer of 1975 the astronaut Neil Armstrong came to visit Swami Muktananda. He told the Swami about his trip to the moon and the wonders of Western technology. Muktananda listened attentively, but a little puzzled until the astronaut finished his tale. The Swami then took a deep breath and closed his eyes for several minutes. When he came back he said to the astronaut, "What took you so long to get there?"

Traveling to the moon on a Wave of intuitive thought or traveling on a highly materialistic spaceship are examples of the two manifestations of Pulse. In every aspect and in every dimension of the self, Pulse is the fundamental organizing principle just as the quantum field is the organizing principle in quantum physics. Our relationship to Pulse shows up in our logic and our intuition. The irony is that many Westerners have taken the astronauts' method of travel to be the only reality. Both ways of getting to the moon are useful, and both take a lot of preparation and practice.

Elements and Music

The question of how elements are created from energy is musically answered by exploring overtones on a monochord in relationship to Sacred Sound. A monochord is a musical instrument consisting of a resonant chamber in the shape of a rectangular box with a string stretched across the box.

When the string is plucked or bowed its sound is amplified by the box. The resulting tone is called the "fundamental." Touching the string at exactly its midpoint will produce a sound exactly an octave above the fundamental. Touching the string at one-third its length will cause it to vibrate in three equal parts, producing a sound a fifth higher still. Touching the string at one-quarter its length causes it to vibrate in four parts, giving a tone two octaves above the fundamental. And touching the string at one-fifth its length causes it to vibrate in five equal parts and sounds a tone a major third above the fundamental, though two octaves up.

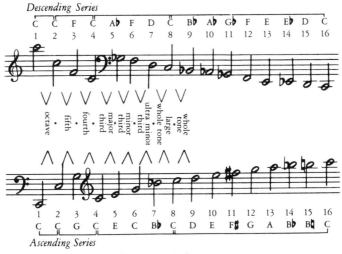

Overtone Series

The sounds obtained by touching the strings are called overtones. The overtone series ascends in whole numbers, i.e.: 1 (fundamental), 2 (octave), 3 (fifth), 4 (octave), 5 (third), 6,7,8,9,...n. Our musical scale can be derived from the musical ratios of the overtone series. For example, 1:1 is the fundamental. The ratio 1:2 creates an octave. Similarly, 2:3 is a fifth, 3:4 the interval of a fourth, and 4:5 the interval of a major third.

By meditating and experimenting with the monochord, Pythagoras explored overtones and their relationship to nature, geometric proportion, and Sacred Sound. The string of the monochord represents the potential of creation. Because it is not moving, it could be imagined as nothingness. The plucking of the string represents the beginning of creation: Pulse, Wave, and Form. The resulting overtones explain the mystery of the one becoming many. All creation myths start with the Word (fundamental) followed by a series of events (overtones): "And a river (fundamental) went out of Eden to water the garden, and from thence it was parted, and became four heads (overtones)." (Genesis:2)

The image of the caduceus with its central staff and two intertwined snakes resembles a high-speed photograph of a vibrating string. The formation of each chakra from Sacred Sound is similar to the overtone series of a vibrating string. The difference is that Sacred Sound descends and the overtone series ascends. The descending currents of Sacred Sound represent involution, stepping down into grosser matter. The ascending overtone series represents evolution, stepping up into higher vibrations of spirit.

Overtone Series

Fundamental (Earth or Heaven). In music, the sounding of the monochord string as a whole is called the fundamental and sometimes referred to as the tonic or home key. The tendencies of all tones is to seek resolution in the fundamental. It is the place to which all sound returns. The classical music composer leads the listener from a fundamental through a series of chords that invariably return to the fundamental. This is another manifestation of the myth of creation. Modern music requires a new way of listening. In breaking from the traditional harmonic journey, twentieth-century composers place the responsibility of resolution upon the listener. That is, the listener, rather then the composer, must create resolution.

Within Sacred Sound the fundamental is not a note or particular pitch as it is in music. The fundamental is in every dimension and every thing, including ourselves. The fundamental is not to be found; rather, the fundamental reveals itself in listening. Healing is always a return to the fundamental. We must seek the fundamental everywhere in our lives. If we are unable to resonate or merge with a part of ourselves, or our environment, we become dissonant or dis-eased. When we become dissonant we beat against or push away from ourselves and our environment. We lose our harmony. Harmony comes from the Greek *harmos*, "to fit together." When we allow ourselves to resonate with something, we are bringing ourselves into harmony with it. The inner experience of this harmony is an experience of our own fundamental.

The sounding board is everywhere. A different way to conceptualize this would be to place a board over all the black and white keys of a piano. Then raise the dampers so all the strings can vibrate freely and press down on the boards, sounding all the tones simultaneously. The resulting sound creates a mass of vibrations that includes fundamental tones, overtones, summation tones, and difference tones. Within this mass of sound the vibrations tend to cluster in specific relationships or ratios. The listener of this event can meditate upon the mass of sound and hear the same intervals we find on the monochord: octave, fifth, fourth, third, etc., generated from "all sounds" rather than just one string.

First Overtone: First Diapason (Ether).

To find the first overtone, a bridge is placed at the halfway spot of the monochord string dividing the string into two equal parts. When either side of the string is plucked the new pitch, when compared with the fundamental, will sound an octave higher. The term "octave" is misleading, especially when related to the first overtone of Sacred Sound. Western music fills the tonal space created by the division of the fundamental with eight tones, hence the term octave. However, in terms of Sacred Sound, it is more accurate to refer to the first overtone of the fundamental with the Greek word diapason. Diapason, literally translated, means "through all" or "through the whole": through the entirety of tonal space. The diapason is to audible sound as Ether is to the elements. Just as all basic element relationships take place within the space of Ether so all basic tonal relations can be found within the diapason. This fact is recognized not only in Western music traditions but in all civilizations of all times.

The diapason represents a cosmic absolute. Just as the division of the string was necessary to create tonal space, so the division of the universe into polarities was necessary to create the world. The Chinese represented this principle with Wu Ch'i and Tai Ch'i. In Sacred Sound, Wu Ch'i is equivalent to the Word or OM. Wu Ch'i is the fundamental represented by an empty circle.

Tai Ch'i is equivalent to the first overtone and is created when the empty circle divides itself into polarities.

To the ancient Chinese the negative and the positive, the dark and the light, heaven and hell, the soft and the hard, the empty and the full, the yin and the yang, all originated from fundamental Wu Ch'i. Polarization is not opposition but complementarity. When the two poles, yin and yang, work together they create a balance. The Chinese believed that the balance of yin and yang was the basis of all healing. Similarly, the biblical story of the Creation begins with the Word which undergoes repeated division: heaven and earth, light and darkness, land and water, male and female, etc. Polarities make possible all life—they are the context within which all problems arise and are resolved. The fundamental is revealed through the merging of polarities. Within the yang there is yin and within the yin there is yang. The first overtone is poetically described by Lao Tzu, the founder of Taoism, in the Classic Tao-te Ching:

> *In order to contract,*
> *It is necessary first to expand.*
> *In order to weaken,*
> *It is necessary first to strengthen.*
> *In order to destroy,*
> *It is necessary first to promote.*
> *In order to grasp,*
> *It is necessary first to give.*

Second Overtone: Fifth (Air Ascending).

The next step is to divide the monochord string by three. With the help of a measuring tape, the string is divided into three equal parts and a bridge is placed at one-third the string's total length. This creates the third overtone known as the musical interval of a fifth. Again, as with the octave, the labeling of a fifth creates some problems. A fifth implies five steps, though the number of steps the fifth is from the fundamental is arbitrary and changes from culture to culture. For lack of a better term, the tone sounded by the monochord will be referred to as the fifth.

The division of the diapason by the fifth represents the spirit of harmony. Lao Tzu wrote: "One has produced Two, Two has produced Three." One of his commentators explains:

> These words mean that One has been divided into
> Yin, the female Principle, and Yang, the male
> principle. These two have joined, and out of their
> junction came (as a Third) Harmony. The spirit of
> Harmony, condensing, has produced all beings.

Harmony is the basis of all healing. The Greek root *harmos* refers to the process of joining together objects, people, concepts, etc. previously having a separate existence. As with many words, its meaning has been obscured by value judgments. The meaning of harmony in music is at best questionable. There are some who believe that Bach creates beautiful harmonies whereas Liszt is non-harmonious and difficult to listen to. There are other people who find harmony in Liszt but not in Schoenberg. Contradictions are necessary in life. Yet everything is harmonious, since it all comes from Sacred Sound.

Third Overtone: Second Diapason / Fourth (Air Descending).

The division of the string by four creates the third overtone which sounds two octaves above the fundamental and an octave above the first overtone. It completes the second diapason of the overtone series. The second overtone divides the diapason created by the first and third overtones into two parts: the intervals of a fifth and fourth.

The fifth and fourth work together as yin and yang. The Tantrists symbolized the relationship of these intervals by the two interlocked triangles of the Air chakra. The fifth and the fourth are the basis of the 1-4-5 chordal progressions found throughout music of all cultures.

Fourth-Seventh Overtones: Third Diapason / Thirds (Fire Ascending and Descending). The division of the monochord string by eight creates the third diapason of the overtone series which contains the fourth, fifth, sixth, and seventh overtones. Within this diapason the intervals of a fifth and fourth are divided: the fifth into a third and minor third and the fourth into an ultra minor third and large second. It is as though the division of the diapason is repeating itself within the newly formed intervals.

The intervals of a third are related to the element Fire. Just as the Air element pulses in harmony with the intervals of a fourth and fifth, the element Fire pulses with the intervals of a third and minor third.

Eighth-Fifteenth Overtones: Fourth Diapason / Seconds (Water Ascending and Descending). The division of the monochord string by sixteen creates the fourth diapason of the overtone series which contains the eighth, ninth, tenth, eleventh, twelfth, thirteenth, fourteenth, and fifteenth overtones. These overtones divide the diapason into seconds and minor seconds. The major and minor seconds divide the thirds, minor thirds, and ultra minor thirds of the third diapason.

Musical Scale

Our musical scale is a reduction of the overtone series into one diapason. The ascending and descending elements found pulsing through each diapason now pulse through the scale as a whole. The intervals of a fifth and fourth are the center, unifying the polar extremes of the diapason. The intervals of a second and third are respectively descending Fire and Water into an Earth fundamental. The ascending second (major sixth) and third (major seventh) are respectively Water and Fire ascending into Sacred Sound.

Interlude

Mind Mist

A Guided Meditation summarizing the principles of Sacred Sound, audible sound, and listening into intuitive language.

Imagine you are entering a mist of very fine droplets. You notice that the forms around you begin to disappear, slowly dissolving, becoming the mist. All around you forms are dissolving into ultrafine droplets of mist.

These droplets of mist are cool upon your body . . . enticing. . . .

You are enticed. Reality as you know it: houses, cars, streets

> *telephones   rugs*
> *the sky   rocks, lakes,   even the ground*

you are standing on slowly become mist. . . . then the planet . . . and further and further into space

> *other planets   asteroids   stars. . . .*
> *everything*
> *becomes mist   fine droplets of mist. . . .*
> *everywhere.*

Your attention turns towards your body as it slowly dissolves into the mist. At first there is some fear, and gradually and safely the fear disappears as you allow your body to lose its physical form and become mist.

Your awareness goes deeper into the mist. You begin to notice patterns arise and disappear among the thousands of droplets.

You realize these patterns are your thoughts. There is a moment

and slowly you let these thoughts go until there is just the mist. No forms, no patterns, no thoughts . . .just a mist going forever in all directions . . .pulsating

> *slowly   outward*
> *and slowly   inward*
>   *mist*

There is a brief memory of your form.

It disappears.

You become mist and there is the mist and there is awareness.

(One-minute pause)

Suddenly within the mist a thought vibrates droplets of mist into patterns of form. It is enjoyable to be so deeply at rest and watch forms take shape so effortlessly within the mist.

As you relax, ever deeper reality upon reality appear and disappear as each rhythmic undulation of thought ripples through the mist.

You are now able to witness the secrets of time as your thought opens gateways. Reality upon reality take form within the mist.

You see the passing of the rise and fall of Rome

the tower of Babylon appears with its magical hanging gardens and you smell the fragrance
you relax with Napoleon and watch Joan of Arc lead her legions

there is the birth and the crucifixion of Christ

*the Buddha appears beneath a tree and holds out the shim-
mering petals of a flower*
you ride with Alexander the Great,

speak with Plato and receive special knowledge

*and now even further back into the world of
dinosaurs. . . . everything . . . every form is knowable
through the motion of awareness within the mist.*

enjoy

Voice Energetics

*The voice is a light. If the light becomes dim, it has
not gone out; it is there. It is the same with the voice.
If it does not shine, it only means that it has not been
cultivated and you must cultivate it again and it will
shine once more.* (Inayat Khan)

Speaking

Speaking is the process of creating an alignment of our words with
Sacred Sound. The rishies, or great seers, of India say:

> *yunajmi vacham saha suryena*
> I yoke the speech to the Sun.
>
> (Tandya 1.2.1.)

When our speech is connected with the Sun, the ordinary sound of
our voice becomes illuminated.

> This speech is the sun itself.
>
> (Shatapatha X.5.1.4.)

Speaking is the movement of Sacred Sound seeking expression. The
alignment of speech with Sacred Sound will enable the listener as well as
the speaker to experience energy and internal freedom. When speech is
not in alignment with our inner self, then there is dissonance, which
causes a dissipation of energy.

The physical process of speaking begins with a thought. When working with the voice the mind must be clear. The speaker must be one-
hundred percent committed to what he or she is saying. Anything less
than that creates dissonance and dissipates the energy of the original
impulse.

One way to check if the mind is clear, is to scan your life and pick one
issue about which you experience uncertainty. It is not necessary to look
for the "big issues." Look for thoughts you repeat that do not ring true,
things you may be saying to yourself or others. For example, you may
really care about whether or not someone calls you, and instead of saying
to yourself or them, "I really would like that person to call," you are
saying, "I don't care." When you have located something questionable,

ask yourself, "Is this what I really want to say?" Ask yourself again and again. If the answer is no, feel free to change both in your thoughts and out loud the sound quality and words to align with your deepest inner intention.

In the beginning of my practice, I believed that when the physical was working correctly, good speech would be automatic. At that time a woman called me and asked me for a relationship counseling session. I was impressed with the clarity of her speech over the phone, and in the initial interview she told me that she was a singer and a voice coach.

The clarity and quality of her voice changed radically whenever she began to say something critical about her husband. Her voice would become constricted and lower in pitch. There was also a sense of pressure and tightness which gave the impression that she could explode at any moment. I asked her to examine her criticisms. She knew they were valid, and yet something was interfering with her ability to express them. With all her voice training she could not get the words out clearly.

When questioning her further, I learned that she had been taught not to criticize her father. When she was a child she had criticized her father, and he had responded by slapping her. After that event she began holding in all her critical thoughts: she did not want to face the pain and fear of another slapping.

I asked her husband, who was present in these sessions, to assure her that he had no intention of hitting her and that he really wanted to hear her criticism. She understood. When she started again to relate a criticism, her body began to shake. I asked her to feel her body shaking, and she realized that she was experiencing the fear and physical pain of the little girl who was afraid to speak out. I asked her then to reassure the little girl inside herself with a clear voice. After she did this, her eyes opened and they were shining. She looked at her husband and began to tell him her criticisms in a very clear voice. Her transformation was amazing. She became powerful, warm, and playful as her voice came into alignment with all the parts of herself.

The change came about through a reorganization of her thinking. A thought when acted upon becomes an impulse in the motor cortex of the brain. It is then organized and transmitted as an electrical impulse to the spinal nerves. These impulses travel down the spinal cord to the nerve endings which affect the entire body, including the physical power-generators of speech, which are the diaphragm, lungs, trachea, and bronchi. Then inhalation occurs in the torso through a complex set of movements. The rib cage expands, and the diaphragm contracts, causing the stomach to move down and the intestines to shift and make room for the expansion of the lungs. The air cells in the lungs then suck in air and this action then prepares to reverse itself in the process of exhalation.

When we have a great deal of muscular tension it can reduce the power of our voice. Thus we find it is necessary to relax the physical body and the muscle groups directly involved with speaking, if we want to speak with power and clarity. It is possible to work with this tension on a physical level by using massage and different vocal exercises, but these are only temporary remedies. If there are mental and emotional factors present, the tension will inevitably return. In Polarity, it is quite common for emotions to come up during a bodywork session. For this reason, a holistic approach is needed.

As can be seen when we examine "The Voice and Its Parts," the stream of air created within the power generators is sent through the bronchi and trachea where it enters the larynx.[1] The larynx houses the vocal cords and is located in the upper part of the trachea near the root of the tongue. The larynx transforms the airstream into sound. As the airstream enters the larynx, a small amount of pressure is built up behind the closed membranes of the voice box. When the pressure is strong enough, the breath pushes on the vocal cords and causes them to vibrate.

Although the vocal cords are the actual sound producers, the larynx is the central organ which organizes the airstream into a specific sonic pattern.

> All the moving forms . . . may be found again in the possibilities of movement of the human larynx. This means that all the movements which Nature uses in the creation of her creatures and also all those movements which, once created, the creatures may use, may be found in the human larynx — as though in a great gathering of creative beings. The larynx has innumerable possibilities of movement, and with every one of them it can delicately influence the stream of breath and impress moving forms upon the flow of air, which then become audible for us as sounds, tones, speech.[2]

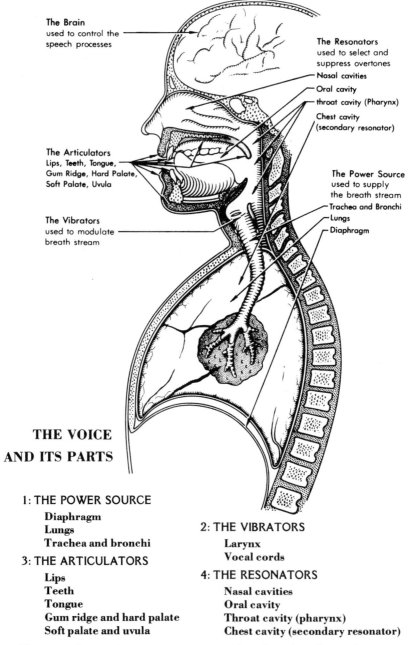

The Brain
used to control the
speech processes

The Resonators
used to select and
suppress overtones
- Nasal cavities
- Oral cavity
- throat cavity (Pharynx)
Chest cavity
(secondary resonator)

The Articulators
Lips, Teeth, Tongue,
Gum Ridge, Hard Palate,
Soft Palate, Uvula

The Power Source
used to supply
the breath stream
- Trachea and Bronchi
- Lungs
- Diaphragm

The Vibrators
used to modulate
breath stream

**THE VOICE
AND ITS PARTS**

1: THE POWER SOURCE
  Diaphragm
  Lungs
  Trachea and bronchi

2: THE VIBRATORS
  Larynx
  Vocal cords

3: THE ARTICULATORS
  Lips
  Teeth
  Tongue
  Gum ridge and hard palate
  Soft palate and uvula

4: THE RESONATORS
  Nasal cavities
  Oral cavity
  Throat cavity (pharynx)
  Chest cavity (secondary resonator)

The vocal cords are two strong bands of yellow elastic tissue stretched across the larynx. The vocal cords open and close in ratios determined by the shape of the larynx. The cymatic pictures on page 58 illustrate sound patterns created by the voice.[3]

The airstream through the membranous folds of the larynx and vibrating vocal cords is transformed into a wave of sound. This sound is then further amplified by what we call the resonators. The resonators for the voice consist of the nasal cavities, oral cavities, throat cavity (pharynx), and secondarily our chest cavity and bones. Speaking of the resonators, Kristin Linklater states:

> The re-sounding of resonating surfaces with the
> body, available to the initial vibrations of sound,
> are virtually uncountable considering that bone,
> cartilage, membrane and muscle can all serve as
> amplifiers and conductors. The harder the surface,
> the stronger the resonance: bone is best, cartilage
> is very good, and toned-up muscle can provide a
> good resonating surface, but a flabby, fleshy, unre-
> sistant area will only muffle and absorb vibrations
> (like a heavy velvet or a sponge). The voice finds its
> most satisfying resonators where there are clearly
> defined hollows and empty tunnels in the architec-
> ture of the body, such as the pharynx, the mouth,
> the nose; but the bony structure of the chest, the
> cheekbones, the jawbone, the acoustically power-
> ful sinus hollows, the skull, the cartilages of the
> larynx and the vertebrae of the spine all contribute
> resonance.[4]

The sound is further molded by the articulators: lips, teeth, tongue, hard palate, soft palate, uvula, and gum ridge. The articulators are located primarily in the upper third of the throat and form what is known as the mask. This term has come from the ancient Greek actors, who actually spoke through masks, which covered part of their faces and amplified their voices.

Morton Cooper writes:

> By producing sound through the mask (as opposed
> to the lower throat alone), the voice opens up,
> becomes flexible, and is filled with expression and
> warmth. It has carrying power and range. Speaking
> through the mask gives the voice oral-nasal reso-
> nance which creates tone focus, which in turn,
> gives the sound aesthetic appeal.[5]

When the articulators and resonators are working in alignment with the vibrators and power sources, the face naturally forms an inverted megaphone shape. Any tightness in the face will displace and weaken the

energy impulse, causing the vocal sound to lose tonal quality and energy. The megaphone-like extension of the facial muscles represents the final transition of the word into the world.

Voice Listening and Notation

Voice energetics is the study of the speaking voice and its relationship to a person's life energy. It involves improving auditory abilities as well as voice training and development through use of a five-element voice evaluation and creating vocal intervention strategies for healing. In short, voice energetics is a method for understanding and evaluating the sound of speech.

The first step in the study of voice energetics is to develop accountable listening skills. Voice changes are an important factor in the energetic evaluation of an individual. The practitioner must be able to hear changes in the speed, volume, pitch, and texture of a person's voice. Once this is accomplished, the relationship of the individual's voice to his or her life energy can be determined, and an "energetic interpretation" can be made.

The next step is to "create a voice" that is flexible enough, or "in tune" with the client's speaking patterns and that will assist in the healing process.

> A doctor coming to see a patient may frighten him and make him more ill if his voice is not harmonious; and another doctor may, by his voice, treat the patient so that before the medicine is brought he is already feeling better. The doctor gives a medicine, but it is the voice with which he comes to the patient that counts.[6]

The following exercises are for the development of listening and speaking abilities. They are similar to a "yoga" for speaking, and require concentration and practice. The rewards are great.

Exercise 1: Changes

Changes is an exercise which must be done in a group of two or three, preferably three people. To begin, one person is assigned the role of speaker, and the other two are the listeners. One of the listeners should also be assigned the role of monitor.

The speaker begins by talking to the listener and the monitor in a "normal voice." It is suggested that the speaker not read from a paper. The content is unimportant. Talk about anything. Just keep talking until the listener and monitor are familiar with your voice. This voice will serve as the median by which changes can be observed. Once a "normal voice" has been established, the speaker will tell the monitor what voice quality he or she is going to change. The speaker must pick one quality to change, either speed, volume, or pitch. The speaker then talks as before, but gradually changing the chosen parameter. The listener must identify the changed parameter through auditory ability. The monitor must validate these changes.

The quality changes must be clear. If a speaker says he or she is going to change speed, then the speed should grossly increase or decrease. The listener should be able to detect the change in speed without being told so by the monitor or speaker. Changing qualities takes practice and concentration on the part of the speaker.

Speakers are quite often unable to control certain qualities. For example, when the speaker chooses to raise volume the speed often increases. The monitor should help the speaker make the distinction between volume and speed and help isolate and differentiate between the different qualities. Initially this exercise may seem awkward, but with practice the changes will come effortlessly.

Exercise 2: Creating a Voice

Creating a voice is an exercise for developing greater listening and speaking ability as well as an introduction to energetic voice notation.

The qualities of speed, volume, and pitch are represented in the following way.

Speed: slow ———————————————————— fast

Volume: soft ———————————————————— loud

Pitch: low ———————————————————— high

In practice the words will be removed, creating something like bar lines in music. When a dot is placed on a line it will represent the value of speed, volume, or pitch. For example:

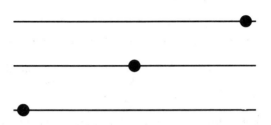

This voice has a fast speed (see first line), medium volume (see second line), and low pitch (see third line).

For this exercise each member of the group creates a voice, drawing three lines and placing dots at the appropriate values. This notated voice is then performed by another member of the group. Once spoken to the group's satisfaction another voice is created, etc.

Exercise 3: Changing Voices

Changing voices is a combination of Exercises 1 and 2. This exercise requires the speaker to change from one voice to another. As in Exercise 2, each group member is responsible for creating and notating voices.

The following new notations of an open circle and arrow show the direction and change of voice qualities.

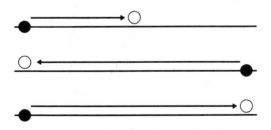

In the above example the speed goes from slow to moderate. The volume changes from loud to soft, and the pitch moves from low to high. When the voice is spoken, the speaker starts with the original voice and gradually changes to the second voice. The group verifies if they were able to hear the notated voice. If not, they must coach the speaker into creating the notated voice.

Exercise 4: Timbre and Elements

The voice is divided into five basic timbres which are related to the presence of elements. Notations for the elements have been added.

○ **Ether**   The timbre of Ether is open and resonant.

✳ **Air**   The timbre of Air is breathy.

△ **Fire**   The timbre of Fire is a sharp and distinct staccato sound.

∿ **Water**   The timbre of Water is connected flowing movement.

☐ **Earth**   The timbre of Earth is a low and deep resonance.

Talk with each other in your group, utilizing each timbre quality. The listener must identify the timbre through auditory ability.

Exercise 5: Prototypes of Element Interpretation

This exercise relates different combinations of elements to timbre, speed, volume, and pitch of the voice. The general relationship of speed, volume, and pitch to the elements is given below.

Speed:	very fast—fast	Air
	moderately fast—medium	Fire
	moderately slow	Water
	slow—very slow	Earth
Volume:	very loud—loud	Air
	moderately loud—medium loud	Fire
	medium low	Water
	low—very low	Earth
Pitch:	very high—high	Air
	moderately high—medium	Fire
	medium low	Water
	low—very low	Earth

These relationships are based on the ultrasonic core and caduceus currents as a continuum of vibrational frequencies from high to low, fast to slow, etc. The qualities are presented in a linear format. In practice their interpretation is more complex. Understanding these general relationships is a necessary step towards voice interpretation.

Each of the following voices should be tried out and discussed. Discussion should include subjective reactions to creating the voice, i.e., images, people associations, as well as any specific body sensations and emotions.

The following additional notations have been added.

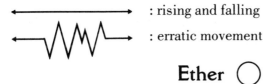

: rising and falling

: erratic movement

Ether ◯

Ether. Ether is space and it has an open, resonant quality. When there is a lack of Ether there is limited vocal expression. The range and flexibility of the voice are restricted. The voice will sound "squeeky." Since all the other elements seek expression through the throat, these elements cannot be conducted when the throat is constricted by a lack of Ether.

Air ✳

Air. The timbre of Air is manifested by a breathy voice. When someone speaks fast and makes quick changes in content we can recognize this as the presence of the Air element.

Air with Fire. (Expansive and Rising or Scattered and Disparate): The speed of the voice is fast and there is a breathy staccato timbre with a

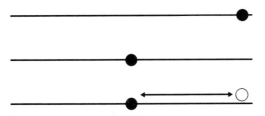

mid-range volume. The pitch starts at mid-range and rises as the Air increases and expands. As Fire consumes Air the pitch will fall back to mid-range.

Air with Water. (Moist and Refreshing or Humid and Heavy) The speed of the voice is fast and there is a breathy flowing timbre. Words seem to

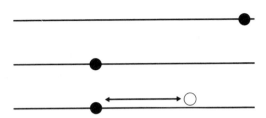

flow into one another. The volume will be low mid-range and pitch may rise to create more Air.

Air with Earth. (Fast and Precise or Dusty to Suffocating): The speed is erratically fast. In this voice there may be a sudden pause and deep breaths, sometimes giving the sense of slowness. However, there is

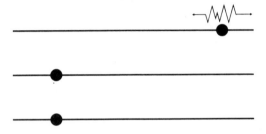

always a sense of speed. Volume and pitch are within the upper part of low range and will vary with the breathing. When the voice is fast and precise, there is a sense of crystallized structures in Air.

Fire △

Fire. Fire has a sharp and distinct staccato timbre. It leaps out. Its primary quality in the voice is volume, which tends to rise without awareness.

Fire with Air (Explosive Flames). Air fans Fire and causes it to increase. If too much Air is added to Fire, the Fire will first die down, and

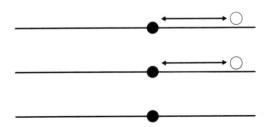

then suddenly increase. The voice begins with a medium to medium-high volume, pitch, and speed; then, if it is followed by an increase of Air, the voice changes by becoming faster. With the increased Air the Fire will leap out, heard as a sudden increase in volume. As the Air is consumed by Fire, the voice returns to its starting point. The staccato timbre of Fire is always present.

Fire with Water (Steam). When Water comes into contact with Fire it creates steam. Pressure builds up like a geyser which may explode at any time. In addition to the staccato quality, the words are controlled and connected. This voice does not leap out, as does Fire with Air. The

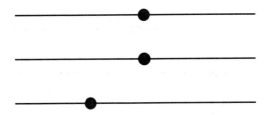

volume is mid-range and very steady. The speed tends to stay mid-range and the pitch drops to Water range. This voice, though it may seem controlled, is very unstable. The Fire wants to evaporate the Water. The voice will increase in speed (Air) erratically so that the Fire can increase. If the Water remains constant, the voice will always return to moderate speed.

Fire with Earth (Glowing Embers). Fire burns Earth. When Earth is burning with Fire it glows and creates a consistent heat. Word pronunciation will be slow and also staccato, staying at medium speed and volume. The pitch is low (Earth). Because of the instability of Fire, the speed and

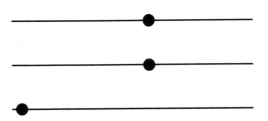

volume may fluctuate (an increase of speed and volume means that there is more Air, while a decrease means there is more Earth).

Water ∿

Water. Water has the timbre of being connected and flowing. A voice that has a great deal of Water lacks substance. The Watery voice will absorb anything. For example, yelling (Fire with Air) causes the voice to become steamy. If Fire is continually applied to Water, it will eventually boil or erupt.

Water with Air (Bubbles or Babbling Stream). The speed varies from medium to fast and the pitch varies from medium low to medium

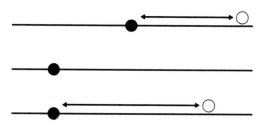

high. The volume is medium low. The image is that of a running stream with bubbles of Air. The timbre of Water is always present.

Water with Fire (Warm or Boiling). The timbre of Water will be present, though less obvious. This voice is warm and flowing with the

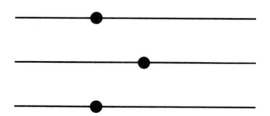

staccato quality of Fire mixed with the quality of Water. One may feel comforted when listening to this voice.

Water with Earth (Cloudy or Nourishing). The Water-Earth voice moves along like a slow meandering river. The pitch is low and the speed and volume are in the medium to medium-low range. The timbre is slow,

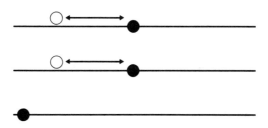

flowing, and connected, and the content of the voice is precise and moving.

Earth

Earth. The timbre of Earth is deep resonant. An Earth voice is low in pitch and slow. It is often the type of voice that gives a sense of support, like an old midwestern farmer.

Earth with Air (Porous). Earth with Air is like a structure through

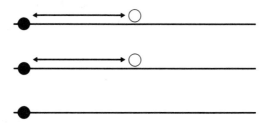

which other elements easily pass. The timbre is slow and breathy. The pitch is low, and the volume and speed are easily changed.

Earth with Fire (Clay). Fire evaporates the moisture in the Earth. It consumes the Air and leaves the Earth dry and crusty, like baked clay.

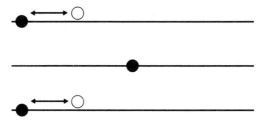

This voice is low in pitch with a gruff and dry timbre. Volume is within the Fire range and the speed and pitch are medium slow to very slow.

Earth with Water (Mud). Water in Earth creates mud which can be either healing or stagnant, depending upon the amount of Air. This is

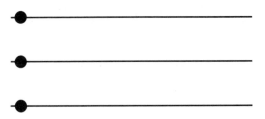

heard as a deep voice moving slowly. Sometimes it will stop, and as more Air is introduced, it can become like wind over the Water as the voice picks up speed.

Voice Interpretation

Voice interpretation requires organizing subjective and objective observations of another's voice into a meaningful whole. The foundation of voice interpretation is participation. Some therapists believe participation leads to attachment, bias, and dependency between therapist and client. An accomplished healing-arts practitioner is willing to work closely with others, conscious of the dynamics of their interaction. Through this participation the practitioner organizes his or her intuitive and objective perceptions into an interpretation. This interpretation is a method for choosing how to work with the client.

It is important here to dispel the myth of complete objectivity. The eighteenth-century concept of observing an objective universe from a distance needs to be updated. The Uncertainty Principle developed by Werner Heisenberg, a Nobel Prize-winning physicist, has shown that it is not possible, even in principle, to measure subatomic particles objectively or with any certainty. Physicist John A. Wheeler writes:

> Nothing is more important about the quantum principle than this, that it destroys the concept of the world as "sitting out there," with the observer safely separated from it. . . . To describe what has happened, one has to cross out the old word "observer," and put in its place the new word "participator." In some strange sense the universe is a participatory universe.[8]

Voice interpretation requires a language of participation. The preceding exercises were designed to develop the initial steps in this language. The following additional information is necessary for making an interpretation.

1. Environmental Context: The speaker's environment and the context of that situation must be considered. Any situation provides an opportunity to study voice energetics: a person talking loudly in a quiet restaurant or a person speaking softly at a loud athletic event.

2. Emotions and Personality Attributes: The following chart represents emotions and personality attributes that can be heard in the voice.

Emotional Qualifiers	Personality Attributes
Happy	Baby
Joyous	Little Boy
Ecstatic	Little Girl
Agitated	Adult
Restless	Parent
Irritated	Victim
Angry	Manipulator
Upset	Calculator
Fearful	Controller
Nostalgic	
Sad	
Lonely	
Grieving	
Depressed	

The emotional qualifiers and personality attributes may be combined; for example, a happy little girl, an irritated manipulator, etc. Persons skilled in verbal counseling often emphasize emotions and attributes heard in the voice to the exclusion of the underlying elemental energy. For example, a sad-little-girl attribute may show up in one person as Water with constricted Fire. In someone else the sad little girl may appear as Fire and Earth with suppressed Water. Having the person "get in touch" with the sad little girl is a metaphor for experiencing qualities of energy that have been avoided. The real healing lies not so much with the sad little girl but with the client learning that she does not have to avoid the energies associated with the sad little girl.

On an energetic level there are no emotions and attributes, just energy in various states of vibration. The composer John Cage stated that sound has no meaning. This is true of the voice. The elemental energies expressed in the sound of the voice have no meaning, morality, ethics, judgments, or memories. Placing these values upon the voice limits a person's physical, emotional, and mental well-being.

It is important to notice emotions and attributes in the voice and to ask, "How are they being expressed?" Ask what element or combinations of elements the person may be avoiding and then seek to create a situation where the person can experience that energy in a safe and creative way.

3. Notice the elements: their interaction with each other, their movements, their presence and their absence. These aspects (qualifiers) are notated in the following way. These descriptions are to serve as listening guidelines.

[ ] *Constriction* is a tightness in the voice and/or throat—lack of space.

( ) *Suppression* is the pushing down of an element. Suppression can be partial or complete, i.e., the element is either entirely absent or only partially heard. The absence of an element does not necessarily indicate suppression. The environmental context must be taken into account.

↓ *Inward Directed* is withheld, as in inner-directed suppressions, or hardly audible.

↑ *Outward Directed* involves projecting outward into the world—highly audible.

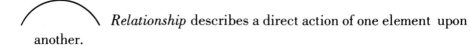 *Relationship* describes a direct action of one element upon another.

Case Study

The following case study is an interpretation. It is an energetic evaluation of an individual in order to show how the preceding exercises may be organized and notated. The notational format is always the same. The qualities of speed, volume, and pitch are represented on top. Beneath are the elements shown in the order of the magnitude of their outward expression. The qualifiers are then added. Underneath the elements, if appropriate, emotions and attributes may be labeled.

This voice is from a man asked to speak about his work, and then his relationship to his wife.

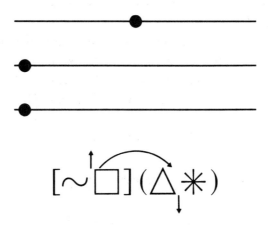

This man is expressing constricted Water with Earth

and suppressing Fire and Air.

He complains of an ulcer with gas in the bowels—suppressed Fire (ulcer) and Air (gas). Emotionally, he feels stagnated and unable to let go—no Fire. He has a lot of well-thought-out ideas and can't put them into action. The ideas represent the creative mental aspect of Water. Earth is shown in the structuring of his creative thinking.

When asked if he ever raised his voice (Fire-volume), he said no, stating that his parents always fought in loud voices. This had hurt him so much that he decided never to be loud like them. His decision placed a judgment-meaning-morality upon the qualities of volume and speed and thus ultimately upon the elements of Fire and Air. These elements became associated with pain and hurt, especially in close relationships. As a result of this childhood decision, he could not express the elements of Fire and Air.

The physical, emotional, and mental effects of placing values upon vocal sounds are complex. The man had to be taught to appreciate Fire and Air in his relationships as an adult. To do this, he had to give up his previous associations concerning those elements. Once accomplished, each life situation involving participation with Fire and Air spontaneously came into balance. He is now free to enjoy the elements.

Exercises

Exercise 6: Interview (Listening for and Interpreting Conversational Changes)

This exercise is done in groups of three. There is one speaker and two listeners. One of the listeners will be an interviewer and will ask the speaker (interviewee) to talk about his/her life.
The interviewer requests that you:

1. Talk about your hobby.
2. Talk about your relationship with your parents.
3. Talk about your vacation.
4. Talk about a close relationship, i.e., spouse, girl/boy friend.
5. Talk about your career.

The interviewee will be given thirty seconds to reply. It is not necessary to finish the answer. Knowing this, he/she should be prepared to stop suddenly. The listeners will notate and interpret the voice. When they are done, the interviewer will proceed to the next question.

When the interpretations are completed, they should be shared. Each listener should talk about their interpretation. If your conclusions are radically different, find out why. Use the discussion to clarify and sharpen your abilities to interpret another's voice. Share your answers with a willingness to be accountable for your perceptions.

The last step of this exercise is to look over your interpretation of all five questions and notice any overall similarities. For example, there may have been some restricted Fire present for question 1 and question 2. Or, there may have been a strong emphasis on Water during all the questions, with very little Fire appearing. Analyzing the results will often reveal important information about the person, which can be used to create a unique healing strategy. After making the data comparison it may be appropriate to ask further questions.

Strategies for Interpretation.

1. When listening to the voice, describe the first thing you notice. For example, this person is speaking loud. He speaks on and on, it takes forever for him to get his words out. That's really an uptight voice or she sounds like an angry little girl. That was really a Fiery voice, etc.

2. Look at your subjective impressions with regard to the qualities of speed, volume, pitch, and timbre.

3. Begin by looking at the most dominant, outgoing qualities. Using your intuition, translate these qualities into elements and notice your subjective feelings and sensations.

4. Ask yourself what was not obvious in the voice. Consider the environmental concerns as well as your subjective reactions. For example, the person is speaking with an obvious Water timbre and volume. Pitch and speed are all in the Water range. However, the environmental context requires more Fire. Where is the Fire?

5. Review your overall impression of the voice, your intuitive perceptions of tightness, freedom, etc., and your logical deductions. For example, a person is speaking in a Fiery voice, which is very loud and staccato. Intuitively you wonder why the Water quality is missing, and then you notice that there is a fear about letting the Water surface.

6. Compose a notation of your interpretation. Look over the result and ask if it fits your experience of this person. If you get a clear yes, the interpretation may be finished. If you get a partial yes or a no, try rearranging the voice emotional qualifiers or recheck your interpretation of the elements until you get a clear yes. Regardless of your doubts or considerations, do make your interpretation with confidence. Trust your intuition and if necessary "confidently pretend." Remember that interpretations are your personal participation records.

7. Ask the interviewee questions that would help you validate your interpretation. These questions may revolve around physical, emotional, mental, and spiritual aspects of the energy qualities you perceive.

Voice Exercise 7: Creating Voices

Each person in the group creates a voice that the rest of the group will interpret. Start with the type of voice you "just can't stand." Then go to the type of voice you really appreciate. Analyze your likes and dislikes of each voice on an elemental level.

Voice Exercise 8: Creating Personal Voices

This exercise involves externalizing how we speak to ourselves and, if appropriate, changing our internal voice. It is suggested that it be done with a partner, although because of the personal nature of the work, it may be done alone. Once the internal voice is brought out it can be evaluated and used to create a balance of elements. This new voice should be safely practiced and gradually integrated.

Your voice is an excellent healing instrument. It is comparable to a set of tuning forks and a shelf full of good music. The voice is a great gift, and with understanding and practice it can be used to create miracles.

Music

*Many say that life entered the human body by the
help of music, but the truth is that life itself is music.*
(Inayat Khan)

Choosing music for healing requires an ability to recognize the elemental qualities of the music as well as the energetic needs of the client. Music that is healing for one person may not be healing for another. For example, the current trend of "new age" music leads one to believe there is a specific type of music that is healing. If one listens to the qualities found in new age music, it would appear that only music which is moderately slow, soft, and low to medium pitch can be healing. New age music, which will be discussed further in this chapter, is generated from the element Water. It is like a water meditation, like ripples crossing a pond on a quiet day. This music can help someone who has spent the day moving at a very fast pace without time to eat or catch his breath (Fire and Air). It evokes Water, slowing down the pace and allowing for more fluidity. But Water music may not be healing for someone whose life is already at a slow pace. Such a person may need to have more contact with the Fire and Air archetypes. It then becomes healing for them to pick up their pace and become more outward and directed, quick and Fiery. Dancing at the disco is more therapeutic for this person than listening to new age music.

It is futile to try and define what kind of music is healing according to one's biases, lifestyle, or values. One cannot say that Bach is more healing than jazz or that new age music is more healing than disco. It is unfortunate and confusing when a particular style, piece, or composer of music is elevated to a healing status to the exclusion of other music. For example, one writer tells us we should listen only to classical music because "all jazz is evil"; another claims impressionists are dangerously sensuous, especially Debussy because he kept many cats! Yet another states that "Jazz is the movement of the soul and the only true American music" and that "Debussy heard the harps of Angels when he composed." These opinions result in fragmented groups of music appreciators who justify and defend their favorite music. Each group develops its own reality, complete with beliefs, philosophies, myths, as well as rules of conduct and dress codes. Imagine how classical, punk, rock, jazz, new age, avant-garde, and reggae appreciators would look standing side by side, each one believing their music was the only music.

Musical style is only a thought attempting to categorize the invisible into a recognizable association. One can understand style, write about style, criticize style, praise style, and agree and disagree about style. Style is a trick, an illusion. We attach ourselves to style as a way of being secure in the face of the unknown, and still music remains incomprehensible.

Music has no value or morals. Music does not think. When music replaces our thoughts we are in trance and are open to suggestion. There is no longer a question of thinking. We are in motion. We are merged as one with the music. Our thoughts, emotions, and physical bodies are moving with the elemental qualities of the sound. Later, the self remembers. Music is always a participatory and energetic event. The difference between what is secular and what is divine in music is only a matter of focus. The divine is always present.

> What music is and is to be may lie somewhere in
> the belief of an unknown philosopher of half a cen-
> tury ago who said: "How can there be any bad
> music? All music is from heaven. If there is any-
> thing bad in it, I put it there by my implications and
> limitations. Nature builds the mountains and
> meadows and man puts in the fences and labels."
> He may have been nearer right than we think.[1]

Music is a force beyond our thought, our culture, and our history. It transcends our associations. All music is potentially healing.

Element Listening

> We have lost something in the areas of human rela-
> tions, compassion, and communication. This loss
> is a consequence of our highly developed technology....
>
> (Max Parrot, M.D., President A.M.A.)

We are exposed to the qualities of the five elements by listening to and playing music. Element listening is a way to understand how music can be used for healing. Learning to perceive the elements in music is a process which involves listening to the qualities of sound, i.e., pitch, speed, volume, and rhythm, and becoming more aware of our physical sensations and responses to the music as well as trusting our intuition. Our experiences are then reviewed and translated into energetic language.

A model for understanding element listening is the division of brain function into left and right hemispheric activities. Although this way of viewing the thinking process is not completely accurate, it is useful. In this model the left hemisphere of the brain contains the rational, thinking, and critical functions. The right hemisphere contains the creative, intuitive, imaginative, and global functions. Western culture tends to emphasize and reward left-brain activity more than right-brain activity. When we begin to trust our intuitions, feelings, and sensations the left brain quickly explains our perceptions, pulling us back into the logical mind.

This is why the right side of the brain has become distant and unfamiliar. Intuitions become unreliable and inaccurate when they are compared to computer readouts, microscopes, and electronic technologies. Under these conditions, our intuitive perceptions are more difficult to trust as valid sources of information. It takes a lot of courage to overcome the fear of being wrong and to allow our right-brain information to surface. Learning to understand this side of ourselves requires that we free ourselves of skepticism and judgment.

Modern medicine relies heavily on the rational mind. Doctors are trained in the sciences and taught to specialize and compartmentalize. Music does not fit into a left-brain dominant medical model. Some medical practitioners are now speaking out in support of the development of intuitive skills. Dr. Irving Oyle states:

> The compulsively technological health professional would like to type your symptom complex into a computer, and have the computer respond like a multiple-choice soda machine, popping prescriptions for the proper pills. Steadfastly thwarting the dream of total automation is the difficult living factor, "the human factor", the psyche of the patient. [2]

While the practice and study of medicine can be criticized for its rational extremism, the practice and use of music healing can benefit from the more rational perspective of medicine. Many people practice element listening without being aware of it. One may be attracted to a certain quality of music and listen to it on the Walkman for hours. Differrent music is chosen for skating, jogging, relaxing, making love, socializing, studying, fighting, etc. When a certain music fits an occasion we know it because it "feels right."

All healing is about bringing a balance between our intuition and our rational thinking. Element listening combines intuition with a rational model of life energy. This kind of listening brings the "art" back into healing. It begins with a gut-level intuition, generating raw information, which is then refined by the mind and expressed as a healing strategy.

Personal Taste

Personal taste includes opinions, feelings, and preferences about music. Element listening begins with understanding personal taste and then transcends these personal musical preferences in order to discover the elements. The practitioner must be in rapport with the client's personal taste in order to make healing music recommendations. For example, if someone prefers rock music, and you believe that only classical is healing, then there will be a problem. You might recommend Brahms or Mozart and tell a person to stop listening to rock music, when in fact their elemental needs may be satisfied with certain qualities of rock. Everyone is different and must be assessed individually on an elemental level as well as that of personal taste.

I once worked with a man who complained of heaviness, inertia, and a lack of motivation in his life. His element picture presented suppressed Water and Fire. I asked him about his musical tastes. He said he listened to slow jazz ballads. I asked him when it was that he developed a taste for this music. He said that fifteen years ago he was very wild and active and had done some "crazy things" (Fire). At that time he only listened to hard rock music (Fire music). Then a friend introduced him to jazz and he felt drawn to it and couldn't explain why, only that it seemed "important."

In terms of the elements, he needed the Watery quality of jazz to "mellow out" from the Fire of the hard rock. In the beginning this music was healing. It helped him to slow down and focus more deeply on issues in his life. After many years of listening to this music, however, his whole life became too Watery. The Water was putting out the Fire. Everything in his life was being organized around the beat of slow jazz. Even his speech patterns changed when he talked about his days of hard rock. His voice became more Airy and Fiery. When he talked about listening to slow jazz his speech became slower and more Watery.

In both cases he went to extremes. Fire and Air are positive yang elements and Water and Earth are negative yin elements. His relationship with his parents was also polarized. When he talked about his mother his voice became fast, loud, and stacatto. When he talked about his father his voice became slow and connected. During childhood he felt split between his parents.

These relationships were parallel to his musical tastes. A healing music for this man would integrate these extremes, loud and soft, fast and slow, and high and low. These extremes needed to be introduced to his listening tastes. Because of his predilection for jazz I recommended that he listen to Gershwin's *Porgy and Bess*. A value judgment based on listening tastes would have led one to believe that the problem was musical style, and yet solutions can be found on an elemental level regardless of style.

Personal taste is sometimes based on personal fears. For example, consider a music that has a moderately slow Water element beat and is felt in the pelvis as an undulating movement. The Water element is involved with sexuality. If the listener has sexual fears held in the pelvic region he or she will never get the beat. They may even condemn the music. Those with similar fears will agree with that value judgment.

Rhythm

> Rhythm and motion . . . are the foundations of musical art.
>
> (Igor Stravinsky)

When we transcend the value judgments of personal taste, we open ourselves up to experience the many different qualities of music. The first and most important quality is rhythm. The basis of rhythm is beat and pulse. Webster defines beat as a "pulse throb" and defines pulse as "to beat or throb as the heart; to vibrate or quiver." In music, pulse throb is like the ultrasonic core — it is the soul of music.

I got rhythm,
I got music.

(Ira Gershwin)

It don't mean a thing
If you ain't got that swing.

(Duke Ellington and Irving Mills)

To understand the meaning of beat and pulse, we must merge with a piece of music and experience how the music moves us before listening to any other quality. Our body must be relaxed and we must be willing to feel the beat inside. Music is perceived kinesthetically; it is not an intellectual process. The body must be free to move and the mind be aware of how it is moving.

The concept of merging with the pulse of the music is important. In science, another word for merging with the pulse is termed "mutual phase-locking of two oscillators," or entrainment. It is a universal phenomenon. Whenever two or more oscillators in the same field are pulsing at nearly the same time, they tend to "lock in" and begin pulsing at exactly the same rate. This demonstrable principle is the axiom of systems theory: the less diversity in a system, the more energy it will conduct. In other words, nature seeks the most efficient state, and it takes less energy to pulse in cooperation than in opposition.

In counseling theory and bodywork, this merging is called pacing or melding. Dr. Upledger explains melding as the basis of efficient bodywork:

> The idea is to "meld" the palpating part of your body with the body you are examining. As this melding occurs, the palpating part of your body does what the patient's body is doing. It becomes synchronized.... If you work with your eyes closed in a quiet state of concentration, there is a good chance that your hand will begin to sense the movement of peristalsis within the patient's upper digestive tract... as well as many other physiological phenomena which are occurring under your hand. The key to success in using this type of palpation is your quiet, non-intrusive melding with the patient.[3]

Entrainment is the basis of counseling and efficient communication. The more one person is in rhythm with another, the closer they will become. This is called pacing or gaining rapport. A counseling student learns how to see movements in another's body and to allow his or her body to move in the rhythm of these movements. The more the student comes into someone else's rhythm, the more he or she will learn about the person. Thoughts, emotions, and feelings will come easily, as if by psychic perception. The practitioner can allow this information to surface through intuition and use it to ask questions.

On every level of life there is rhythm and entrainment. During the movie *The Incredible Machine* two individual muscle cells from the heart are seen through a microscope. Each is pulsing with its own separate rhythm. As the cells come closer together, they begin to pulsate in the same rhythm. During relationships when two people are "in love" they appear to pulsate together. When immersion into the pulse of love is interrupted with arguments the couple always goes out of phase.

Pulse is the basis of the ultrasonic core and gives rise to the yin and yang energies of the caduceus. As described earlier, the vibratory movement of the two snakes creates centers of energy called chakras. Each chakra has its own pulse and qualities known as the elements of Ether, Air, Fire, Water, and Earth. They are universal and can be found in the human body-psyche as well as in music, nature, speech, etc. We must be free to dance with the rhythm of the elements. We can then merge with the rhythms of the cosmos. Our mind as well as our body becomes a resonant sounding board for spirit.

The general relationships of rhythm to the elements is as follows:

Earth   Very Slow—Slow
Water   Moderately Slow—Moderate
Fire   Moderately Fast—Fast
Air   Very Fast—Erratic
Ether   Silence—Space

Once a feeling for rhythm is achieved, the next step is to listen for the qualities of speed, volume, and pitch. Exercises in listening for these qualities are explained in depth in the chapter on Voice Energetics.

Speed:	very fast—fast	Air
	moderately fast—medium	Fire
	moderately slow	Water
	slow—very slow	Earth
Volume:	very loud—loud	Air
	moderately loud—medium loud	Fire
	medium low	Water
	low—very low	Earth
Pitch:	very high—high	Air
	moderately high—medium	Fire
	medium low	Water
	low—very low	Earth

Element events take place throughout all music. To perceive these events it is necessary to pay attention to the interaction and changes of the qualities shown above, along with the underlying rhythm. This makes listening exciting! For example, the underlying beat may be Fire, while the speed, volume, and pitch may increase to Air, and then drop to Water. This is common in many works of Beethoven. There is a Fire drive that reaches up for Air and falls back to Water and Earth only to reach up again. Beethoven's music tells an element story: the element of Fire explodes into Air, burning itself out and falling back into Water, only to rise back up to Fire again.

Perceiving archetypal events in a piece of music requires active listening. The mind must be present to perceive quality changes rather than to judge the music. Some pieces of music will be easy to categorize and others will be more complex. For example, blues and new age music each have different qualities, yet they both share the Water element. Because of its slow-moving connectedness with moderately low volume and pitch, blues can be likened to a deep pool of water, sometimes dark and swampy. This is a perfect environment for expressing deep emotions. In contrast, new age music is like contemplating the surface of a body of water. The Water beat is always present, but the qualities change faster than blues and the pitch levels are higher. This creates the effect of ripples across water.

It is interesting to analyze Muzak from an elemental point of view.

Lee Valvoda of the Muzak Corporation describes Muzak:

> We are usually compared with music, but that is
> not our purpose at all. It's easier to describe what
> Muzak is not rather than what it is. It is not
> background music and it is not piped music and it
> is not entertainment music. Because it is used
> specifically and entirely for commercial purposes,
> we call it functional music. [3]

The function of Muzak is to create environments for shopping, waiting, working, and eating. To accomplish this the company picked popular music compositions which bridge age, race, and lifestyle. The pieces are rearranged in formula fashion: the beat is slowed down, volume is always reduced to very low, and drums and vocals are usually removed. A string section is often added. The connected Watery qualities of each piece of Muzak are emphasized by the gliding of the strings. The strings also serve the important purpose of accenting pitch in the medium to high range. This helps to balance the reduced volume level.

The aim of Muzak is to get the listener to identify with the music. The vocals are left out, leaving the listener free to fill in the words. This is usually done unconsciously, with memories or experiences associated with the music. It is important that the music appeal to our positive experiences and associations. The shopper feels secure in an Earthy environment, but not suffocated because of the high-pitch quality of the strings (Air). The Watery quality, emphasized by the gliding of the strings, is relaxing and contemplative, encouraging us to create uses for the many products we can purchase. Muzak is further enhanced when subliminal suggestions are embedded in the music. For example, "purchase now" or "you will be happy when you buy." The Muzak Corporation is well aware of how to use music to get results. It is unfortunate that their insights are used for questionable purposes. It is not surprising that the Muzak Corporation slogan is: Music is art. Muzak the science.

This is an example of understanding the power of music and how it can be used to manipulate people into spending money. It is to the financial advantage of the makers of Muzak to keep the public ignorant about music. The more auditorily unconscious we are, the greater the impact of Muzak. However, we must become more responsive to our sonic environment. It is possible to listen attentively to Muzak. Anything less than that is like walking through a forest with our eyes closed.

Once element listening is developed, one is then able to recommend healing music to another. The element needs of an individual are evaluated through analysis of voice, physical symptoms, expressed needs, and intuitive perceptions. This information is assembled into an element picture. For example, a friend asked if I could recommend music that would help him "settle down." He worked in sales and had a tremendous amount of drive. His voice was Fire with Air. The only physical symptom he complained of was restlessness. It was clear that he needed a music that would appeal to his Fire qualities and lead him to Water. Because his personal taste was classical, I recommended the Great Symphony of Schubert and Beethoven's Op. 111 piano sonata. In making this recommendation I recalled my element experiences of each piece and matched them with the element needs of my friend. A similar process is employed in choosing music for different occasions such as parties, dances, etc. We are constantly making these decisions on previous conditioning. With element listening, the process is more accountable, and we are able to make clearer choices.

Spontaneous Improvisation

> Do attempt to bring greater harmonies into the
> experience through the practice and through the
> application of self in making music. Even though it
> may be only on a comb or on glasses or on bells, on
> a harp, violin or a piano, MAKE MUSIC!
> (Edgar Cayce reading)

Spontaneous improvisation is the experience of making music for well-being. It takes no specialized training beyond our life experience to make sounds. The only requirement is that we have a willingness to do so. Everyone, regardless of his or her musical training, has the potential to enjoy creating music. Anything that makes sound is a possible instrument: pots and pans, spoons, table tops, hands clapping, as well as pianos, drums, bells, etc. No formal training is needed to improvise. It is unfortunate that many people have lost touch with music because of their self-consciousness or fear of being criticized. Three quarters of the world's population enjoys creating and dancing to music and yet has no idea how to read music. As the composer Gustav Holst says, "Personality no longer counts for anything, and when that happens, music begins."

If we choose to play in a particular style such as classical, folk, or jazz, then we can channel our energies to make sound through an established school. However, when we look into the roots of all musical styles, we discover people improvising. Joseph Haydn talks of improvisation:

> I would sit down and begin to improvise, whether my spirits were sad or happy, serious or playful. Once I had captured an idea, I strove with all my might to develop and sustain it in conformity with the rules of art. [5]

The act of creation is always childlike and innocent, regardless of age and culture. Everyone can create a sound and experience self-expression. I have watched many people, including myself, look deep into their hearts, and without formal training allow a sound to emerge. During my years as a therapist, I have watched many people express themselves through music who couldn't relate verbally, and who had little or no formal music training.

I recall a woman who was afraid to play the piano because she was told she didn't have a musical ear. I asked her to forget the idea of a musical ear and sit in silence, tuning into her feelings. After I assured her that no one in the room knew anything about music, she began to play loud, then soft, fast and slow. One could hear her emotions in the sounds and see the physical changes in her body as she expressed herself through the piano. From the standpoint of classical harmony, it would have been judged as bad music. However, from a musical perspective beyond style and rules, she played wonderful music. We all applauded because her honesty and her courage moved something inside of us.

A good way to begin improvising is to become familiar with the sonic potential of your environment. Stand in any space and begin turning. Look at objects, i.e., walls, rugs, tables, radiators, rocks, glasses, mud, etc. and imagine the sound they could make. Then begin looking a second time and when some object appeals to you, begin tapping, rubbing, knocking, hitting, or scraping it. Next begin humming with the sound. Allow yourself to merge with the sound. When you have thoroughly explored that sound, allow yourself to go on to another object. When working in groups, people are encouraged to share their favorite sounds.

When beginning to improvise as a group, it is always a good idea to tune into your individual sound first. Allow your sounds to mingle and intertwine with other sounds in the room. As this happens a special group awareness emerges. Paul Hindemith said that "people who make music together cannot be enemies, at least while the music lasts."

The following are some possible ideas and structures for spontaneous improvisation groups.

Children's Toys and "Noise Makers". A child's world is filled with sound objects. Every toy store has a special section filled with children's instruments and noise makers. Devote an improvisation session to these sounds.

Kitchen Sounds. Have everyone bring in pots, pans, forks and other utensils from their sonic explorations of their kitchens.

Trash Sounds. Have everyone bring in sound objects from the street that others have discarded.

Instrumental Sounds. Explore and play traditional music instruments without concern for what they should sound like. Let your imagination be your guide. For example, rather than play the black and white piano keys, it may be more interesting to open the top and pluck the strings.

Recording. As you become more comfortable and secure with exploring sounds and creating music, you may want to record your sessions for further enjoyment. You can then listen back on your sessions and ask questions about the elements manifested in your music.

Graphic Scores. Using a piece of paper, large or small, allow your body to react to real or imagined sounds by drawing lines. Ask the group to sing or play your score.

Composing

We all have an individual and social responsibility to restore our personal and collective universe to a state of integrity. Regardless of our life-calling, whether it be composer, garbage collector, business person, doctor, or priest, the responsibility remains the same. According to Don Juan, a Yaqui Indian sorcerer:

> Any path is only a path, and there is no affront, to
> oneself or to others, in dropping it if that is what

your heart tells you. . . . Look at every path closely
and deliberately. Try it as many times as you think
necessary. Then ask yourself, and yourself alone,
one question. . . . Does this path have a heart? If it
does, the path is good; if it doesn't, it is of no use.[6]

When the composer's vision is clear, the resulting vibration of the
work will serve and support healing.

The wind blows over the lake and stirs the surface
of the water. Thus, visible effects of the invisible
are manifest.

(*I Ching*)

In this general sense all composers are healers. Within this context
one might question the intention of Muzak, advertising, and other profit-
oriented media that employ music. I believe that the word composer
should be reserved for those who create music from their heart.

The art of improvisation and composing are lifelong processes.
Everyone should be involved in making music. It is exciting and always
an adventure. May you all make music!

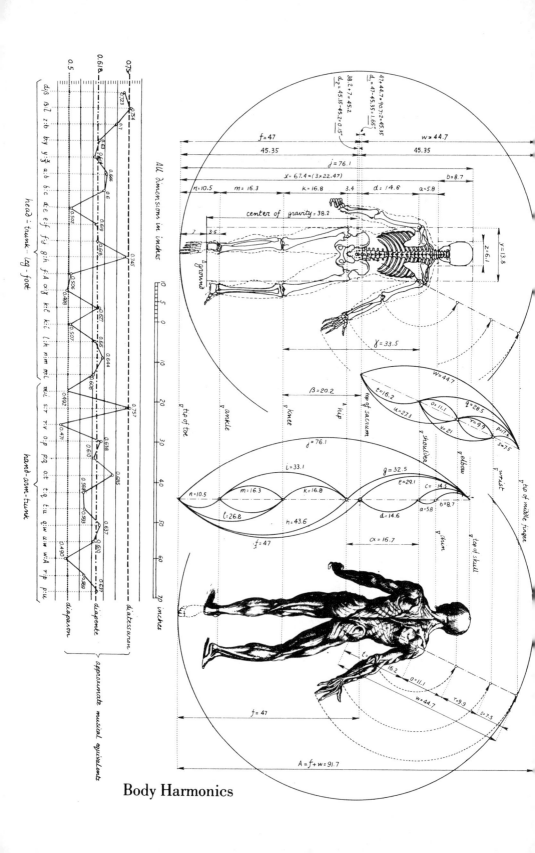

Body Harmonics

Tuning Forks

Tuning forks provide a simple and effective method for activating the overtone series in meditation and healing. Listening to pure Pythagorean intervals is a method of attunement with Sacred Sound. Through the act of tapping two tuning forks together we can hear Sacred ratios. These ratios are found in nature and are considered by the ancients to be a fundamental part of the human soul or psyche. Each interval can potentially awaken within us a deep universal archetype. We can understand this best by first looking at the theory of resonance.

Resonance occurs when the vibrations of one object reach out and set off vibrations in another object. The word "resonance" comes from the Latin verb *resonare*, meaning "to return to sound." If the two objects have identical frequencies and one is vibrated, the other object will also sound. For example, if you have two tuning forks of the same pitch and you strike one, the other will also make sound. This is called "sympathetic resonance." Forced resonance occurs when the primary vibration is transmitted by force to some other object. For example, the vibrating string of the piano forces the wood of the sounding board to vibrate, regardless of the respective frequencies. As a result, the tone of the played string is intensified. Without the help of the sounding board, the vibrating string would be audible, but very weak.

The intervals of the tuning forks create a sympathetic resonance with the quality of Sacred Sound deep within us. The archetype begins to align our thoughts and physical body around its vibration. For example, when the forks are tapped, it is quite common to observe the head and body move and adjust to the proportions of the sound. This is a form of forced resonance. Our body and mind become a sounding board for Sacred Sound.

If we look at our bodies as actual manifestations of the patterns of Sacred Sound, we can begin to understand how the sound of the tuning forks can be used for healing. The diagram at left demonstrates human harmonics.[1]

Body harmonic ratios can be determined by dividing the smaller distance by the larger distance and relating the fraction to a musical interval. For example, in the diagram here, the distance from the extended toe to the coccyx is 43.6 inches. The distance from the top of the coccyx to the top of the head is 32.5 inches. Dividing 32.5 by 43.6 equals the ratio .745, which is musically equivalent to the interval of a fourth.

The geometric alignment of the physical body is a healing method used to bring an individual back to the proportions of Sacred Sound. A good bodywork practitioner is trained to "eyeball" a person's body, to look at the proportions and relationships between different body parts. If someone's shoulders are raised, and his hips pulled forward, the practitioner learns to associate this posture with a mental attitude or the tendency for certain organs to be weak. For example, in Polarity we use the pattern of a five-pointed star as a guideline for healing. Dr. Stone refers to the star as nature's geometric keyboard. Its mathematical proportions are the same as the intervals of a fifth and fourth.

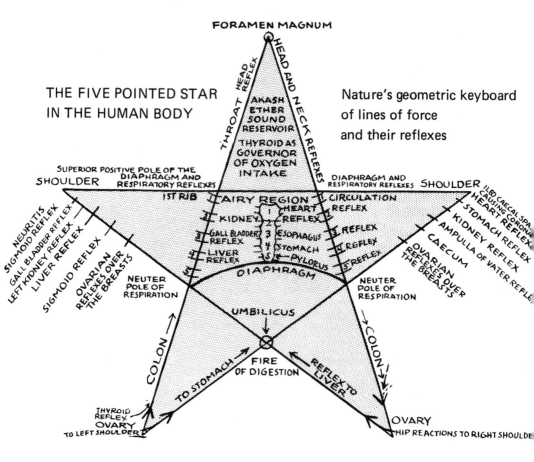

Pressing points along the diagonals of the star harmonizes dissonant lines of force, which interfere with the expression of the intervallic proportion on a physical level. When we feel physical pain, or when our bodies feel numb or tight, there is dissonance and the body is out of alignment with Sacred Sound. If the points are sore there is a corresponding dissonance in the mind, and there may also be a weakness in the organs through which the line of force passes. By allowing the client to feel and relax into the pain, it is possible to regain a sense of harmony. The person is gently guided into a more flexible harmonic pattern. The client experiences harmony as well as being-awareness and relaxation. To be aware and relaxed is experienced as a continuum ranging from calm to excited relaxation.

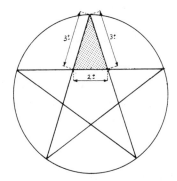

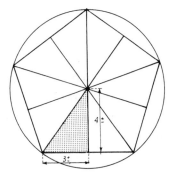

Diapente – or 2 : 3 – corresponds to the sides of the pentagram's triangle, approximated by 2 : 3 = 0.666... ≅ 0.618 = φ

Diatessaron – or 3 : 4 – corresponds to the pentagon's triangle, approximated by a 3-4-5 triangle. 3 : 4 = 0.75

An excellent way to explore body harmonics is to use a tape measure and measure the distances between joints on different people. After a while the tape measure will give way to your internal sense of proportion. Remember that the body is meant to be flexible and mobile, like good music. If you detect areas of rigidity, then the harmonics related to that area are not being expressed. It is possible to recommend tuning-fork intervals related to the harmonics of the blocked area in order to assist the restoration of muscle tone.

A deeper key to understanding how overtones and music work on a physical level is to examine the relationship of body harmonics to the fluctuation of cerebrospinal fluid and craniosacral therapy. The anatomical term "sacrum" derives its name from the latin *os sacrum* which means "sacred bone." Proper harmonic alignment of the sacrum with the feet and head creates the intervals of a fourth at the coccyx, a fifth at the second fused bone of the sacrum, and a sixth at the top of the sacrum. This opens an area an inch and one half below the navel referred to as the Tan Tien in Taoism. Freedom of sacral motion and harmonic alignment of the sacrum is optimal for the production and fluctuation of cerebrospinal fluid. CSF was considered by the ancient Taoists to be the physical counterpart of Chi or life energy, and more recently by cranial osteopaths as the elixir of life. Dr. William Garner Sutherland, founder of Cranial Osteopathy, states:

> The cerebrospinal fluid is the highest known ele-
> ment in the human body. . . . He who is able to
> reason will see that this great river of life must be
> tapped and the withering field irrigated at once or
> the harvest of health is forever lost.[3]

Intervallic proportions have a direct effect upon the craniosacral system, which in turn affects our central nervous system and posture. The tapping of the forks directly affects the central driving mechanism of cerebrospinal fluid which is known to the osteopaths as the primary respiratory rate. Dr. Magoun defines the primary respiratory rate as:

> . . . the name given to that metabolic and regulatory
> complex which is considered to be fundamental to
> life itself. One cannot help but to make the connec-
> tion between the pulse of the primary rhythm
> and the pulse of the ultrasonic core. In this
> anatomical-physiological mechanism is included
> the inherent motility of the central nervous system,
> the fluctuation of the cerebrospinal fluid, the guid-
> ing and restraining action of the intracranial and
> intraspinal dural membranes, the articular mobil-
> ity of the cranial bones and the involuntary mobility
> of the sacrum between the illia.[4]

A powerful technique for affecting the primary rate and balancing the craniosacral system is to induce a "still point" or, in musical terms, to return to silence. Dr. John Upledger describes a still point:

> The total craniosacral system motion (primary
> respiratory rate) will "shut down," i.e., become
> perfectly still. . . . During the still point, everything
> relaxes. . . . The breathing becomes very relaxed.
> Any muscle tension seems to melt away. . . . The

still point may last a few seconds to a few minutes.
When it is over, the craniosacral system will
resume its motion, usually with a better symmetry
and a larger amplitude.[5]

When we listen to intervals produced by the tuning forks we stimulate our vestibular nerves. Our vestibular system is the basis of our sense of space, proportion, and balance. When we induce a still point with tuning forks, it is hypothesized that the walls of the ventricles (choroid plexes) change their physical proportions to reflect the ratio of the applied interval. The new proportion is optimal for secretion of CSF and balance of the intracranial dural membranes. This in turn harmonically organizes the motion of the individual cranial bones with the sacrum and the sound of the central nervous system.

Listening to Your Nervous System

The direct effect of the tuning forks upon the cranial system can be felt with skilled palpation. Although learning to feel the primary rate is beyond the scope of this text, an exciting alternative is to listen to the auditory effect of balancing the primary rate upon your nervous system.

The composer-philosopher John Cage related a story in his book *Silence* about discovering the sound of his nervous system. This story inspired me to explore the sound of my nervous system in the anechoic chambers at New York University. An anechoic chamber is a completely soundproof room. Much to my surprise, hearing the sound of my nervous system was familiar. I had heard it while meditating and on quiet nights before going to sleep, as well as during times of unusual stress. After repeated visits to the chamber I began to listen for changes in the sound.

The pitch of the sound would change, depending on the events of the day and my internal state. For example, if I was calm my nervous system would make a low, even, soft sound. However, one day after having an argument with a subway attendant I noticed the sound became much higher, louder, and that it wavered radically. Over a period of several months I began to associate physical, mental, and emotional states with the sounds of my nervous system. During this period of deep listening I was able to detect two separate sounds simultaneously occurring in my nervous system. I became sensitive to the sound of my nervous system outside of the chamber and to the effect of outside events upon it. I read the following story in Manely P. Hall's *The Therapeutic Value of Music* which made me become more aware of how one could consciously use sound to tune the nervous system.

> A demented youth forced his way into the dwelling
> of a prominent judge who had recently sentenced
> the boy's father to death for a criminal offense. The
> frenzied lad, bearing a naked sword, approached
> the jurist, who was dining with friends, and
> threatened his life. Among the guests was a
> Pythagorean. Reaching over quietly, he struck a
> chord upon a lyre which had been laid aside by a
> musician who had been entertaining the gathering.
> At the sound of the music, the crazed young man
> stopped in his tracks and could not move
> (stillpoint). He was led away as though in a trance.[6]

I then began to experiment with the overtone series by using tuning forks tuned to Pythagorean intervals. I listened to my nervous system while tapping different intervals in the anechoic chamber. As I suspected, my nervous system attuned to the interval.

I already knew that many auditory nerves pass from left to right and right to left within the human brain.[7]

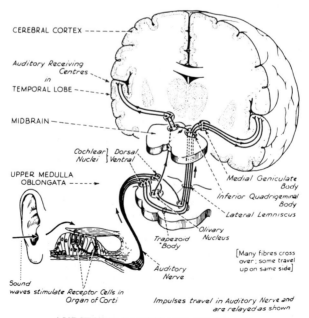

AUDITORY PATHWAYS TO BRAIN

The intervals, when viewed on an oscilloscope, present patterns that are reminiscent of the crisscrossing of the caduceus as well as the crisscrossing of the auditory nerves. [8]

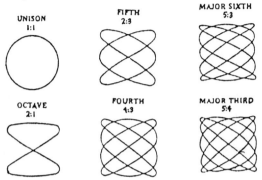

When I first stepped out of the chamber into the lab, my nervous system still held the interval within it. It was as though my left and right brain were cooperating, a feeling which I later came to understand as a balance in cerebral functioning. As I moved among the people and animals in the lab, the tuning of my nervous system began to change. After a while I began to notice how my nervous system changed according to the different life situations I was in. I then realized that the tuning forks could be used as meditative teaching devices which could reawaken ourselves to simple and accessible energies.

Healing and Meditating with Tuning Forks

The use of tuning forks in healing and meditation involves three components: extension, intention, and reception.

Extension is the *method* of producing sound. Extension involves understanding the tuning-fork system. The forks must be tuned to Pythagorean intervals as follows:

C=256 cps	=1	1/1	Earth
D=288 cps	=2	8/9	Water
E=320 cps	=3	4/5	Descending Fire
F=341.3 cps	=4	3/4	Descending Air

G=384cps	=5	3/2	Ascending Air
A=426.7cps	=6	3/5	Ascending Fire
B=480cps	=7	11/12	Ascending Water
C=512cps	=8	1/2	Ether

These tunings are based upon a mid-range sound comfortable to the ear. A numbering system has been added to assist the non-musician in choosing intervals. The elements' archetypes are based upon the relationship of the overtone series to Sacred Sound as explained in the chapters on Music and Elements. Any interval can be picked by referring to the number 1 plus the number of the interval wanted. For example, the interval of a fourth (4) is number 1 plus number 4. The interval of a sixth (6) is number 1 plus number 6.

Tuning forks are available in aluminum and steel. The aluminum tuning forks are easier to use, as they vibrate longer. Although they do not have the subtlety and pure tone of the steel forks, they are more versatile.

Upon receiving a set of aluminum forks, find a safe and quiet place to experiment. Lay the tuning forks out in the order shown above. Sit in a comfortable upright position. Start with the octave (forks 1 and 8). Holding the forks by the stems, tap them on your knees or on the floor.

Hold the vibrating forks about one to two inches from your ears.

In order to be sure you make a sound, hold the forks by the stem and tap them firmly. The aluminum forks will make a clear audible tone which lasts twenty to thirty seconds. It is better not to tap the forks together because this will cause a ringing sound that is inappropriate for use directly in the ear.

The extension phase of the tuning forks is complete when you have learned how to make the intervals and how to tap the forks so they create a sustained, even sound. The following order of initial experimentation is recommended:

1. Octave (1 plus 8) Blue
2. Fifth (1 plus 5) Blue Green
3. Fourth (1 plus 4) Green
4. Third (1 plus 3) Yellow
5. Sixth (1 plus 6) Yellow Orange
6. Second (1 plus 2) Orange
7. Seventh (1 plus 7) Red Orange

Colors can also be added to the room in the form of light bulbs or theater gels, in order to make the environment more conducive to healing. The colors in the chart correspond to the color frequencies of each element.

Another method is to tap the aluminum forks and move them around your head. The forks should be tapped twice, which will create a loud ringing sound. Then the forks should be circled around the head. The motion should range from slow to fast, always keeping the forks two to eight inches away from the head. You should be in a sitting position.

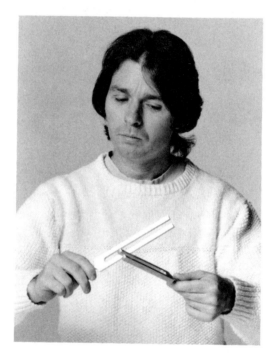

When extension is mastered the intention phase begins. Intention is your intention for the sound. The intention to heal has to be clear before the forks are tapped. The practitioner must relax inside. Once the tap is made, the forks rise to the ears like a floating dance. The mechanical concept of tapping the forks only to get the sound will not work. The sound interval must become a messenger for a deeper archetypal experience as amplified by the intention. The following story illustrates this point.

When I was a student at Indiana University I happened to be in the music auditorium one afternoon. It was the afternoon of a piano concert to be given by Rudolph Serkin. The piano tuner was tuning and I was enjoying being the only one in the hall. Since it was dark off stage and I was in the back of the hall, I found it easy to dose off to the tuning sounds. I remember at one point the piano tuner striking middle C over and over. I must have heard him play it thirty or forty times. Then there was a period of silence for two to three minutes. I drifted off in the silence.

Then out of the silence I heard middle C again. This time the note sent shivers up my spine. The sound was completely different and at the same time I knew the note was the same. Then I heard it again and again. It was like a concert—there was something very special about this middle C. I opened my eyes and to my surprise I saw the piano tuner standing next to the piano. And sitting at the piano playing middle C was Rudolph Serkin.

When tapping the tuning forks our intention is important! The intention carried by the sound can be picked up by everyone present. This is expected from any good performer. It should never be a mechanical process. The healing arts are a profound communication with oneself or others. The intention to extend oneself to another is the key to healing.

Receptivity is the art of preparing to receive the extended intent. It is important to have the skills and sensitivity to know how to receive sound and to share that ability with others. One way of creating receptivity and focusing intention between people is through the use of guided imagery. Tapping the forks for someone is a special experience. One person may be lying down, while the other holds his head and speaks clearly, creating a story that is special for them and appropriate to their life experience.

After a bodywork or Polarity session, when the client is already in a relaxed state, a story may not be necessary. Perhaps you need only say: "You will be hearing a sound. Just allow your body to relax deeply into the sound and learn what is has to teach you."

The way to select the best intervals for the optimal healing of a client is to assess the client in terms of his or her elemental needs and body harmonics. When choosing intervals to tap, the practitioner may want to create an "element concert" which emphasizes the elements needed. Just relax and allow your creativity and musicality to make a special event for the person receiving the intervals. Remember that the ancient art of storytelling was always accompanied by the playing of intervals on a lyre.

Interlude

Mountain Temple

The Mountain Temple is a guided journey to a Greek dream temple where one receives initiation with Pythagorean intervals.

Imagine you are walking up the side of a mountain. The pathway is winding upward. The air is cool and fresh, and the sun is warm. You can hear the sound of your footsteps and feel the sun warming your body. One step follows another as your breath relaxes into an easy rhythm and you see the pathway winding up from below and the green landscape stretching out, touching a distant lake.

Your attention returns to the upward rhythm of the winding climb, watching the path turn slightly left then curving gently to the right, now feeling the sun at your back. For a moment the sun disappears into the shadow of a large rock, as you turn left again winding even farther up the side of the mountain and nearing the top as the path takes another sharp turn to the right where the sun illuminates and reveals a white temple built into the side of the summit above the clouds. The temple has six white pillars which face the end of the winding path and eleven white pillars overlooking a cliff. You walk towards the temple feeling the increased warmth of the sun as it reaches its zenith, with each step more excited as you near the entrance. At the three marble steps you take off your shoes and prepare to enter. The floor is pleasantly cool to your feet.

Within the temple there is another row of four pillars. You can see across the floor to still another row of four pillars near the far end of the temple. Slowly you move towards a pillar within the outer entrance pillars. Something about this pillar attracts you.

As you reach the pillar you know it is time to sit down, and you do so cross legged, your back resting comfortably against the pillar, the coolness of the floor drifting pleasantly up through your body.

Relaxing, you exhale and see across the temple floor a very old woman dressed all in white. The temple is twelve pillars by seven pillars, and she sits at the intersections of three from the left and four inwards. She is wrinkled with a deep wisdom in her face.

She knows something of the utmost importance. Somehow you know her, she is inside of you and yet she is sitting far from you. She is calm, and the silence of the temple seems to encompass her.

She gestures to you and effortlessly raises two bells. It is time to close your eyes and listen.

Listen. . . . (tap tuning forks)

And as you come back from the sound, knowing and remembering in a safe way, and having learned something of the utmost importance, it is time to return. There is no more to be said.

Thank the wise lady —she nods. You know you can visit her at any time, and the temple is there for you in your dreams.

Mantra

When the mind becomes attuned, it becomes capable
of hearing the voice of the unknown. The sounds
which are heard in such a state do not belong to any
particular language, religion or tradition.

(Swami Rama)

The word mantra has been associated with Eastern religions, gurus, mystic powers, and enlightenment. Mantra comes from the Sanskrit verb *man* which means to think, contemplate, or meditate. A mantra is a "sound thought" that is used in contemplation and meditation.

The underlying principle behind the creation and use of mantras is simple: Experiences are transmitted through sound. Mantras are used in everyday language to communicate inner experiences. Some examples of these mantras are: aha, ummm, ech, yum-yum, mmmmmmmmmm, aaah, and ssh. Children's comic books are filled with mantras: zoom, blam, pow, splat, zing, boom; again, these are sounds that communicate an inner experience. The sound "aha," taken as a word, could have thousands of meanings. It is an inner experience of the speaker in sonic form.

The use of the mantric principle with sounds like aha, ummm, ssh, aaaah, etc., is called "toning." Toning sounds are based upon feelings and sensory experience. They have the ability to create physical and emotional flexibility and are integral to well-being. Toning is discussed further in the next chapter.

This mantric principle is also used by spiritual teachers for the transmission of revelations. Mantric sounds are drawn from insight and awareness gained during deep meditation. The origin of mantric sounds is beyond feeling and sensory experiences. When a person is in deep silence the mind witnesses a soundless sound in the form of a mantra. A mantra which transmits this spiritual awareness is elevated to the level of Shabda or Sacred Sound.

Shabda, a Sanskrit word, is the mantric language of Sacred Sound which has the potential for awakening the archetypes of Sacred Sound within the listener. The transmission of Shabda from a spiritual teacher to a student over a period of centuries is known as an oral tradition. The source of every oral tradition is based upon the inner awareness of the spiritual teachers of that tradition.

An oral tradition dies when the repetition of the mantra can no longer be elevated to the level of Shabda because the inner knowledge is lost. A good indication of a dead tradition is when its followers become rigid and dogmatic about the pronunciation, spelling, and usage of the mantra. A tradition is revived only when the archetypal source of the mantra can reemerge. Mantras that have been revived are alive and flexible. Dr. Pandit Arya, a Sanskrit scholar, describes his experience after receiving a mantra from his teacher Swami Rama. Swami Rama represents a five thousand year-old oral tradition of meditation:

> Sometimes when Swamiji has taught me a mantra,
> the Sanskrit scholar's ego in me has objected to its
> inaccurate Sanskrit grammar or diction. His
> response is that mantras do not go by the rules of
> any language. "This is the way the sound is. . . .
> Accept it as it is given."[1]

It is difficult for a Westerner to understand mantras. The religious context and the rituals and beliefs conflict with Western Judeo-Christian culture. Although the Eastern instructor, whether a Swami, Lama, or Buddhist priest, may insist that the mantra is not associated with any religion or culture, the person receiving the mantra will most often associate it with the religious tradition of the teacher. The student will feel the need to imitate the rituals and practices of another culture in an attempt to experience the mantra. Sometimes the students are actually told they cannot become enlightened unless they follow the religious rituals and practices prescribed by the teacher. Confusion arises when the students fear they will lose their enlightenment if they do not strictly adhere to the practice of their mantra.

Another difficulty concerning mantras is the lack of practical information about how they work. The uninformed student may be prone to superstitions such as: the wrong mantra could in some way be damaging to him, or that only certain people are qualified to know the exact pronunciation of the mantra. Once the principles of mantras are understood it becomes obvious that the physical sound of a mantra is harmless. It is the intention of the giver and receiver which empowers the mantra. Sounds can be used to harm others, in the same way that a hoe, which one uses to tend the soil in a garden and thus used contributes to the growth of plants, can also be used as a weapon to hit someone. The hoe is not good or bad. It is merely a vehicle for the intention of the user. The intention of teaching mantras in this text is for healing; making whole and complete. When the intention of the mantra is service and healing, any mantra that is given to someone else will contribute to that person's growth.

The following story illustrates the relativity of pronunciation: Two monks were crossing a lake in a rowboat. One monk was instructing the other in the pronunciation of a mantra. The monk kept pronouncing it wrong. When they got to the other side of the lake he finally learned the correct pronunciation. They parted company and the monk who had learned the mantra was happy and walked off. The other monk began rowing back across the lake. When he had gotten to the middle of the water he felt a tap on his shoulder. He turned around and there was the other monk standing on the water. The other monk said, "What was the exact pronunciation of that mantra?"

Another belief is that the mantras must be kept secret or they will lose their power. Many people keep mantras secret out of fear. There are, however, valid reasons for not revealing a mantra. A mantra properly transmitted is a deep and subtle experience shared by people who truly appreciate its value.

The importance of secrecy is summarized in this story: A student received a mantra from his teacher who told him that it was a very special mantra that would enlighten souls. He was told the mantra must be kept secret or his soul would be sent to hell. The following morning the student went into the town and gathered everyone around him. When he had the attention of the people he told them the mantra. His teacher, hearing this, asked the student, "Why did you do this after my warnings?" The student replied, "My time in hell is a small price to pay for the saving of all these souls!" The teacher praised him.

There is much to learn from the great spiritual teachers of the East. Sometimes their abilities seem supernatural. They have passed on a special gift wrapped in an exotic package. It is now time to let go of the packaging and start using their gift to heal ourselves. This requires taking responsibility for the principles underlying mantric transmissions, so that we can align ourselves with the elemental energies that are evoked by the sounds. Anyone who is willing to serve another can learn to create and give mantras.

Bija Mantras

> The bija-mantras are the most potent of all. They
> definitely belong to no language and are not found
> in any dictionary. They have no gender and declen-
> sions. They are combinations of letters that repre-
> sent the relationship between the kundalini (life
> energy) and the Supreme Consciousness (Sacred
> Sound), and their specific rays (elemental
> archetypes). . . . An attempt to understand them
> intellectually will be futile.
>
> (Usharbudh Arya)

The mantras presented in this text are the bija mantras of the chakra energy centers. Bija means "seed." The bijas of the chakra energy centers are those "seeds of sound" that are associated with the element of each chakra. The adjacent chart shows the bija sounds in relationship to each chakra.[2]

The bija mantras are combinations of these seed sounds that evoke elemental archetypes for healing. There are thousands of possibilities for creating bija mantras. The following is an example of how a bija mantra is created from the chart.

Through the process of verbal inquiry and energetic voice analysis, an individual is evaluated and interpreted as having "constricted Water with a lack of Ether." The practitioner chooses to work with Ether to open the constriction, Fire to bring out the heat (evaporating excess Water), and Earth to fuel the Fire as well as structure the Water. The practitioner might choose a mantra like "edasa" or "htava" for this person. Both mantras have the ability to open Ether with the seeds *e* or *h*, activate Fire with the seeds *da* or *ta* and fuel Fire while stabilizing Water with the Earth seeds *sa* or *va*.

The bija system uses vowels and consonants comparable to the prin-ciples of yin and yang. Vowels represent feminine energy and consonants represent masculine energy. Some mantric systems found in the Middle East and West favor consonants and sometimes eliminate vowels. The vowel sounds were probably eliminated from the mantras in order to guard against or conceal the feminine principle.

Transmission

Bija mantras can also be thought of as poetic music. An artistic spirit is necessary for the creation and transmission of these mantras. Those

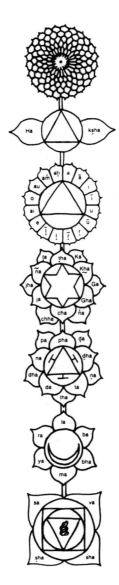

who have developed artistry through music, painting, poetry, dance, etc. will recognize the process in the transmission of bija mantras.

Step 1. Environment. The environmental setting must be safe and secure. Parties, dinner tables, rooms with TVs, stereos, and/or radios playing, or rooms where people walk through unannounced are not good environments. The practitioner should ask if the environment is conducive to relaxation. "Is this environment a special place where deep and important experiences can happen?"

Step 2. Assessment. Through questioning, voice analysis, and intuition, the practitioner chooses an elemental strategy. The elemental assessment of an individual and elemental strategies are covered in the chapters on Voice Energetics and Elements.

Step 3. Creating a Mantra. The bija mantras are organized in two or three seed formulas. The order of the element seeds will be from above to below as shown in the chart. For example, based on an individual's energy assessment, the practitioner chooses to work with Air and Water. The mantra "tamba" is created. This mantra has two elements in descending order. They are *tam* (Air) and *ba* (Water). Or during an assessment of another individual, three elements are chosen: Ether, Air, and Earth. The mantra created, "ainamsa," has three seeds. The first is *ai* (Ether), followed in descending order by *nam* (Air) and *sa* (Earth). When creating three seed mantras the first seed must always be Ether.

When the practitioner has assessed the elements and understands the above order of mantric formulation, the next step is choosing the seed sounds. This involves artistry and intuition. There are no set formulas for choosing specific seed sounds for any element. To create a bija mantra, the practitioner must first go inside and make contact with the elements chosen. This is done by visualizing, feeling, hearing, and thinking about the quality of each element chosen during the initial assessment of the individual. The practitioner's awareness then merges with the individual's, by his or her intention. When this happens the qualities of the chosen elements may change. The practitioner then acknowledges this shift and evaluates the new quality. The evaluation requires an intuitive response to the question, "Is this quality for the highest good of the individual?" The answer may cause the practitioner to make yet another change. A question is raised again and again until there is resonance.

Once you have found the correct quality, the next step is to choose a mantra which resonates with that quality. This is done by whispering or inwardly pronouncing each seed, so that the one that has the most resonance with the quality of the element will be chosen. The seeds combined in the proper order (mantra) are again whispered or inwardly pronounced until the mantra is fine tuned, so that it can resonate with the elemental energy.

Step 4. Seed pronunciations. The following gives the pronunciations of the seeds shown in the preceding Bija-mantra chart. A tape is also available with the pronunciations (see Appendix 3).

Earth va—sa (sah)— sa (say)-sa (shaw) //Ruby//Red
Water ba—bha—ma—ya—ra—la //Pearl//Orange
Fire da—dah—na—ta—tha—da   (day)—dha   (dhay)—na
        (nay)—pa—pha //Coral//Yellow
Air gam—kham—gham—nam—cam—cham—jam—jham—nam
        (am)—tam—tham—kam //Emerald//Green
Ether m (om)—o—r (rat)—u—e—c (ch)—a—i—j (jar)—ai—s
        (ss)—u—a (ah)—s (sh)—h (house) —au //Moonstone//Blue

The above pronunciations (with associated gem and color archetypes) are approximations, and can be helpful in creating mantras. The actual mantra given may be different from what you have practiced because the final mantra is beyond any mental process. It is a sound empowered with Shabda. Swami Rama once said the following to a person who was confused about the sound of a mantra:

> When you gave the mantra, you were a divine being. Now you are thinking of it in human consciousness. Let the divine being do what it must do and you, the mere human, not interfere with it. Whatever mantra came at the time was not yours and is not yours to change. [3]

During mantra transmission the whole experience of the healer is amplified. The deeper the healer trusts the vibration of the elements the more empowering the mantra will be. In transferring a mantra, the whole being becomes a sounding board. Repetition of the mantra will reactivate the experience of the elements for the recipient. The sound of the mantra, however, without the empowerment of the practitioner, is an empty shell.

Step 5: Preparation to Receive the Mantra A guided story is created, incorporating the elemental qualities of the mantra. With the recipient sitting in a comfortable chair, with eyes closed, tell the following story to transmit an Ether-Fire-Earth mantra, "enasha": Imagine that you are walking across a spacious field of blue (Ether) and yellow (Fire) wild flowers. The sun is nearing its zenith and is warming your body

(Fire). The smell of the warm earth is pleasing to your self (Earth). And as a butterfly lands on a wild flower, yellow sunlight (Fire) reflects off its slowly moving wings in a ruby red glow (Earth). Relaxing now even deeper... as the butterfly lifts from the flower and circles your head... naturally and effortlessly perches on your left ear and whispers a special sound

enasha.

When the story is completed, the recipient is asked to whisper the mantra back to the practitioner. This may happen several times. When both of you are satisfied with the pronunciation, the recipient is instructed to go inside and allow the sound to come effortlessly and spontaneously, like a butterfly flying from one flower to the next. He is told to let the sound drift inside him. The essence of the instructions is to tell the client to relax with the sound rather than repeat it mechanically.

Step 6: Bringing the Recipient Back, and Future Use of the Mantra. It is important to allow the recipient enough time to absorb the experience. This can be flexible. Five to fifteen minutes is recommended.

At the appropriate time and in a gentle direct way, the practitioner asks the recipient to come back from the experience. He may say, "It is time to return; allow yourself to use this sound in your dreams tonight." Or he may say, "It is time to return now. Feel free to come back, knowing you can return to the sound at the appropriate time."

When the recipient returns, the practitioner may choose to suggest further use of the mantra. One way is to sit quietly, recall the mantra and drift with the sound. Another way is to repeat the sound effortlessly while drifting off to sleep.

It is suggested that bija mantras be used for no more than two weeks and no longer than ten to fifteen minutes per sitting. This is because the elemental energy may change, and a new mantra may be needed. If the practitioner wants to create a mantra that can be used for a longer period of time it is suggested that a special bija mantra of two or three Ether seeds be created. For example, the mantra "aim."

Interlude

Rain Forest

A Guided Meditation revealing the source of mantric sounds from nature.

Imagine a village located in a valley by a stream that meanders down from mountains covered with a canopy of luscious green trees. The climate is subtropical.... You feel the sun and welcome the cool of the evening.

The water is clean and fresh. Everyday you listen to its sounds ...sitting for hours ...listening ...remembering ... until your parents call and its time to return.

The small village seems so busy.... People moving everywhere.... dusty roads and the smell of cooking from the clay houses.

For many years now the stream has been speaking, telling stories of the mountains, and you have been listening. Listening so deeply that even you do not remember in any normal way, and yet the feeling lingers in your body.

Something is calling.

One day you go to your parents and tell them it is time to follow the stream. They smile because they understand. Saying goodbye is special. It is time to leave the village. It is time to walk deep into the forest. It is time to discover.

There is a dirt path along the stream that leads out of the village. You begin walking. The road is busy with people walking to the next village. You walk together, without speaking, noticing the activity, the movement.

From your left the stream speaks in your ear.

For a whole day you walk along until you come to a bridge. At the bridge the road continues away from the stream to the next village. The people pass across and disappear as the road winds around a rock.

You pull aside a hanging limb of an overgrown tree and discover a small pathway into the forest near the right bank of the stream. You begin walking this pathway.

Step after step the pathway meanders along the stream and then deep into the forest. As you walk the memories of the village and the people on the road begin to fade into the sound of the stream. The forest grows denser. Everything becomes part of the forest.

The pathway becomes smaller and for many days and many miles you meander along the valley floor between the mountains. The moon and stars come and go and the sun changes colors and shades across the forest floor.

One day the pathway begins to climb. The valley is ending or beginning and you feel the upward momentum of the climb. The pathway becomes rocky. With each step the stream appears and disappears under rocks into the ground, first to the left, and then to the right. There is a thought it may be lost. And yet you keep walking up the now steep and somewhat difficult grade, trusting the stream will be there even though the voice of the water has gone deep into the ground.

Then one day the land levels out and you come to a clearing surrounded by a canopy of trees. Standing alone in the center of this clearing is a large tree. Its trunk is very wide and you can see its roots sunk deep into the ground. It is a very old, almost ancient tree, and you feel the urge to rest beneath this tree.

You walk across the clearing and sit down, allowing your back to meet the trunk of the tree. It is warm and inviting and a deep comfort comes over you as your eyes close. A dream comes. You go inside the tree and follow its roots hundreds of feet into the earth. There you discover your friend the stream. It is a wonderful reunion.

Enjoy this for a while.

(Pause)

Coming back from the dream you notice that the full moon is illuminating the forest floor around you in a pale bluish white light. The smell of the warm earth is everywhere and the sounds of the forest are rich. How long you have been there is a mystery now. How many days, months, or years have gone by?

Each day your listening becomes more and more sensitive. There is the sound of the smell of the earth. A sound that changes as the sun bakes the ground. There is the sound of the breeze through the canopy of trees. The sounds of the morning dew rolling across the tops of plants.

Then one day on your right you hear a tiger emerging from out of the forest. At first there is some fear but the fear quickly passes. He walks slowly up to you and begins to lick your right ear, creating a special sound. At the same time you notice a doe to your left. She walks across the clearing to your left ear and begins licking. Her tongue is different and the sound carries a different message. Together they reveal the secrets of the forest.

Listen

When you return from listening, the doe and tiger have disappeared. It is time to follow the stream back to the village. Walking back down the mountain path is easy. You come to the road by the bridge. There are people walking along the road. They notice you and look into your eyes. They want to know about the forest. You whisper the sounds of the forest in their ears.

Toning

Toning is the simple and natural process of making vocal sounds for the purpose of balance. Everyone practices toning. When tired, we tone ourselves with a yawning sound. When in pain we tone ourselves with a scream or perhaps a moan. Sadness is expressed through the toning sounds of crying and happiness is expressed through laughter.

To be free to make sounds is an integral part of healthy functioning. Fully expressed sounds are powerful and effective balancing mechanisms. Imagine touching a hot iron and not making a sound. Without the release of sound the body would tighten. Sound is necessary for restoring the body's balance.

Toning sounds are sounds of expression and do not have a precise meaning. In the process of learning language, most adults underestimate the importance of making spontaneous sounds. Children are excellent examples of uninhibited toners. They have a natural intuition and playfulness around sounds. Listen to children engrossed in play and you will hear a symphony of toning sounds.

Our language is rich with words that depict toning:

yawning	moaning	crying
grunting	panting	breathing
groaning	humming	sniffling
whistling	sighing	gurgling
screaming	laughing	farting
sneezing	sobbing	clearing throat
belching	cooing	gasping
whining	yelping	
snuffling		

One does not have to be a trained musician to make toning sounds like yawning or groaning. In toning there are no judgments, mistakes, or rules. It is a matter of freeing the body and letting the sounds emerge naturally and spontaneously.

The first step in learning how to tone is to work with the toning sounds already present in your life. Notice your yawning sounds and feel them vibrate in your body as you stretch. Notice that yawning sounds have no specific meaning; they are not words, and they are difficult, if not impossible, to spell.

Meaning makes no difference to a sound. For example, "I yawned" is different than "I yawned because I was tired." Allow yourself to enter the sound of the yawn fully as it vibrates through your body. As your awareness of all your toning sounds increases, let the sounds become more exaggerated.

Once you have exaggerated your sounds, expand your repertoire of toning sounds. One basic assumption of toning is that the freedom to make sounds is directly related to freedom of expression in other areas of life. By doing voice exploration, it is possible to reestablish the intuitive, uninhibited expression that we once knew as children.

Voice exploration can be practiced in individual or group settings. Begin by assuming a comfortable position. It does not matter if you are standing up, lying down, or sitting, as long as you are relaxed. Close your eyes and begin making sounds. Begin exploring how different sounds feel. Play with the rhythm and duration of the sounds. Notice how loud and soft sounds affect you. Do not criticize or compare yourself with anyone else. Whatever sounds you make are perfect. Just let them be, and notice how certain sounds evoke feelings or experiences you may have forgotten or avoided. Explore the "ugly" as well as the "harmonious" sounds of your voice—snorts, clicks, sniffles, pants, screams, sighs, hums, chants. Enjoy yourself. It is your journey. You are the creator. You have complete control. Repeat what you like; stay as long as you like in each sound. *There are no rules.*

Exploring sounds in a group is an excellent opportunity to listen and learn new toning possibilities. Someone in the group will inevitably make sounds that are different from yours. A sound that you have resisted may surface in a group situation. You are free within the group to reproduce and explore that sound. During voice exploration there is no need to give reasons for making sounds. Just make sounds and listen. The sounds are the teachers, and the lessons are learned as the sounds emerge, spontaneously and effortlessly.

When a degree of confidence is obtained with individual and group toning sounds, the following exercises are recommended. As your familiarity with the basics of toning grows, you can create your own exercises. These exercises are variations of the toning principle.

Exercises

Exercise 1: Emotional Cycles

sadness	anger	powerful	boredom
fear	happy	lethargic	excited
ecstatic	terror	tense	joyous
contemplative	sexy	mean	love
hate	jealousy	euphoria	empty
despair	full	funny	

Pick any emotion. When working with a specific emotion, sit calmly and begin by holding a mental picture of the emotion in your mind. Pretend that a sound is surrounding and merging with the mental image. Let the sound grow and become more vivid until it penetrates your entire body. Then make the sound. Do not try to be correct. Allow the sound and any accompanying body movements to come freely. Notice the emotions that may be difficult to express and keep them in mind for further exploration.

Exercise 2: Pitch Resonation

Pitch resonation is the harmonizing of sounds of an external instrument, such as a piano, guitar, or set of tuning forks. When choosing a particular pitch for toning, let your intuition be your guide. What is happening? How does it feel? Where is it vibrating in your body? Can you sense yourself inside the sound? At different times in your life, certain pitches will be more attractive than others.

When making the sounds, relax your body, especially your jaw and tongue. Let the sounds rise up inside of yourself as though they were conducted through a hollow tube. Be sure not to tense your throat.

Exercise 3: High-Low Toning

High-low toning is an excellent method to increase your vocal range and to open up new areas in the body. Prepare for high-low toning with belly laughing. It may seem awkward at first, but let go and keep laughing for at least two minutes. This will relax the diaphragm. When you have finished laughing, place your feet in the following manner:

Relax, and gently bend your knees and bring your right hand over your head without tensing.

Visualize a high pitch and let the pitch emerge as though from a hollow tube. Slowly shift your weight from the front leg to the back leg. At the same time drop your arm and lower the pitch. The pitch will follow the hand, moving down the body from high to low.

When you have reached your lowest pitch hold it, and let your body bounce on with the sound.

Exercise 4: Two Person Toning

Sit with another person and have a conversation with sound.

Exercise 5: Toning in the Shower

Sing with the warm shower; switch to cold water and respond with sounds.

Exercise 6: Toning and Bodywork

Note: Anyone working with toning while pressing sore spots should be a qualified bodywork practitioner.

In bodywork practice toning can be used to reduce pain in areas where the energy is blocked. Locate a painful spot and ask the client to imagine a sound that resonates with the pain. Press the point, and as the client exhales ask him to make his sound. You can harmonize vocally with him. The pain may lessen and go away. The same principle of imagining the sound of a painful area may be practiced without actually touching the point.

Exercise 7: Toning with Vowel Sounds

Vowel sounds resonate different areas of the body. The following chart gives the correspondences between vowels and different areas of the body.

Head Cavity	I
Throat and upper chest	E
Chest cavity (also body as a whole)	A
Abdomen (to navel)	0
Pelvis and lower body	U

Polarity practitioners will often press the twanger tendon in the ankle in order to evoke these sounds. The practitioner chooses a vowel for a specific area, and then has the client breathe and exhale with the tone of that vowel, while he's pressing on the tendon. (Note: the twanger tendon, when properly located and pressed, is always sensitive.)

Environmental Toning

Environmental sounds are sounds audible within our immediate sonic environment, such as horns, train whistles, screeching, planes, machinery, water dripping, children playing, phones ringing. These sounds are often labeled "noise" and are considered by some authorities to be pathogenic. William Stewart states that noises of twentieth-century living are major contributing factors in cardiovascular problems and must be considered hazardous to the health of people everywhere.[1] Dr. Lester Santag, in his study relating noise to the unborn fetus, presents scientific evidence to conclude that loud noises, especially the sonic-boom, can cause congenital malformation.[2]

In a two-year study conducted by William C. Meecham and Neil Shaw at UCLA's school of engineering and applied sciences, the death rates in two communities near the Los Angeles airport were compared.[3] One community lived directly under the flight path, and the other community was eight miles away. The researchers found a substantial increase in mortality rates in the communities near the airport. They then concluded, "It appears that the terrible noise that people experience causes a substantial increase in tension which causes tension-related diseases such as strokes."

The studies on "noise pollution" continue. Some state that outside noises impair childrens' development of language and communication skills.[4] Others point out that half of the working population may be exposed to noise levels equal to or exceeding the safe limits for unimpaired hearing.[5] In the area of sleep research it has been found that deep sleep can be cut short by the passing of a single truck; this can cause a deprivation of the dream stages which could lead to psychic abnormalities such as aches, pains, fatigue, depression, and psychotic states.

In another sense, however, noise pollution is energy that can be transformed into healing energy. Although research indicates that the "normal" person is inadequately prepared to deal with these new environmental sounds, it is nowhere proven that these sounds are inherently pathological. If they were, then everyone tested would be affected, and this is clearly not the case. What the research demonstrates is that most people are auditorally unaware: they have no idea of the power of these sounds. Instead of approaching these sounds with awareness and respect, they resist them. And when our bodies resist sounds, they tighten, creating dissonance, or disease.

In effect, "noise pollution" is a subjective value judgment placed upon a sound or a combination of sounds. What may be noise to one person may be pleasing to another. I took a group of New York City college students to a YMCA camp in the country. The students couldn't sleep and were quite disturbed and agitated. I asked them what was wrong and they said there was "too much noise": They were referring to the birds and insects! They were used to sleeping with the sounds of horns, whistles, and sirens.

It would be ideal if there were rubber wheels on subways, less horn honking, and no more tire screeching. A quieter environment may be something to work towards, but in the meantime we have to live with the sounds that are here. It is better to work with these sounds than to struggle against them. With the correct information and skill, it is possible to turn a harmful situation into an exciting energetic experience.

Converting environmental sounds into positive energy experiences requires the understanding of two concepts. The first concept, called "resisting," means fighting against a sound that is interfering with your life. For example, a teacher ignoring the sound of a loud jet while lecturing strains her voice in order to be heard. The students strain to hear her and the outcome is a stressful situation.

The second concept, "mental attitude," illustrates the mind's power to create reality. There is a great deal of support in the world for a negative attitude towards environmental sounds: such sounds are not musical; they are unwanted; they have no beauty; they are dangerous to our health. The collective mind believes these attitudes and empowers them. For instance, we cross a street and see a truck coming. We know the truck is running a red light, but we refuse to get out of the way because of a thought, "The truck has no right to break the law." Our attitude may be right and we may be in the hospital because of it. The same situation exists with mental attitudes about environmental sounds. These sounds are with us, and whether they have a right to be here or not, we cannot avoid them. Children who haven't learned mental attitudes about environmental sounds have a special ability to enjoy them. They love the sounds of tractors, planes, subways, trains, air hammers, creaky doors, etc. We adults also have this ability; we have only to give ourselves permission to listen like a child; permission to forget the important activities of the day and enter into the unavoidable reality of a sound.

There are two methods of working with environmental sounds. The first method involves voice and body movement. When the environmental sound appears, let your voice imitate the sound and let your body be moved by the sound. For example: A car horn suddenly honks and you notice that your body tightens. Your mind is judging the driver and your emotions are held in. This situation is similiar to touching something hot without letting out a sound. Therefore, instead of holding the sound, jump back from the car, allowing your body to unwind the tension and then allow your voice to make a loud spontaneous "honk!"

The second method of environmental toning is called "relaxed listening." During listening you have the power to resonate with your sonic environment. Suspend your mental attitudes, relax, and open yourself to the energy of the sounds. The deeper the relaxed listening the more there is to be discovered.

Environmental sounds can be exciting concerts when properly approached. Everyone enjoys the patter of rain on a roof. The greatest environmental concert in New York City is riding the #1 IRT subway into the South Ferry stop. When the train enters the station it creates a very high-pitched sound. Relax with that sound and listen deeply. It is a gateway into an alternate reality.

"Noise pollution" interferes with classroom teaching, street conversations, hospitals, sleeping, and relaxation. While everyone could be more conscientious about creating a quieter sonic environment, it is not realistic in the near future to expect tractor-trailers to stop running, cars to stop honking, and planes to stop flying. Therefore, let us be more conscious of our present sonic environment and learn to resonate with what we have created. Life will be easier, more vibrant, magical, and childlike.

Appendix I

New Music, New Healing

The healing arts, like the musical arts, are undergoing a revolution. Just as there is a new music, there is a new healing. Speaking of the new healing, Dr. Larry Dossey states:

> . . . The spacetime view of healing and disease tells us that a vital part of the goal of every therapist is to help the client toward a reordering of his world view. We must help him realize that he is a process in spacetime, not an isolated entity who is fragmented from the world of the healthy and who is adrift in flowing time, moving slowly toward extermination. To the extent that we accomplish this task, we are healers. [1]

For the new healers, the accomplishment of this task is through consciousness. In traditional medicine the focus of health care is on the physical body. Consciousness is a secondary and irrelevant factor. In the new healing this assumption is no longer accepted.

> Everything is alive. There is nothing in principle, therefore, preventing the use of consciousness as a primary form of therapeutic intervention at all levels of matter—from the subatomic particles through molecules, cells, tissues, organ systems, etc. [2]

The assumption of this article is that new music is opening the doors to a new way of being—that the experience of listening to new music can alter our world view and change our consciousness and thereby transmute our physical form. . . . And furthermore, that this transmutation is necessary for our next step in evolution, as well as living completely in our current reality.

Defining new music is elusive because the listener is the music. When the listener is "in self" and willing to go everywhere, without hesitation, totally involved and multi-dimensional without regard to any preconceived form (including his physical body) then it would be fair to say that all music is new music.

New music by way of the composer, composition, and performance challenges the listener to maintain his sense of self while being involved in a nonlinear multi-dimensional event.

New music is teaching and preparing us for a universe described by Einstein as "an aggregate of non-simultaneous and only partially overlapping transformation events." John Cage expresses it this way in his Experimental Music Doctrine:

> Urgent, unique, uninformed about history and
> theory, beyond the imagination, central to a sphere
> without surface, becoming is unimpeded energeti-
> cally broadcast. There is no escape from its action.
> It does not exist as one of a series of discrete steps,
> but as transmission in all directions from the field's
> center. It is inextricably synchronous with all other
> sounds, not-sounds, which latter, received by
> other sets than the ear, operate in the same man-
> ner.[3]

Entering new music with our ears—listening—we seek harmony. Not harmony in the tonal sense, but harmony in the original meaning of the word, "to fit together." We learn to let ourselves fit with and resonate with the sounds. Dissonance means not fitting. Dissonance is an inability to be flexible. It is the root of all disease. The physicist David Bohm speaks of health as the essence of nonobstructed, indivisible, flowing movement of the self's internal harmony transcribed into the external world. When the internal and external are at odds with each other— dissonant—the result is disease or a break in harmony. In tonal music the appreciator sought the fundamental in the music as a metaphor of spiritual unity, the ending of a journey. In new music one seeks the fundamental in one's self; the return to the fundamental is anywhere, anytime, and any dimension, because the fundamental is everywhere and here.

> Locations and times—what is it in me that meets
> them all, whenever and wherever, and makes me at
> home?
> (Walt Whitman, *Leaves of Grass*)

> Wherever we are, whatever we hear is mostly
> noise. When we ignore it, it disturbs us. When we

> listen to it, we find it fascinating. The sound of a
> truck at fifty miles per hour. Static between the
> stations. Rain.[4]

This is perhaps the most challenging aspect of new music, that the listener must not only appreciate the sound but give him or herself to the sound. John Cage says that sound:

> ...does not view itself as thought, as ought, as
> needing another sound for its elucidation, as etc; it
> has no time for any consideration — it is occupied
> with the performance of its characteristics: before it
> has died away it must have made perfectly exact its
> frequency, its loudness, its length, its overtone
> structure, the precise morphology of these and of
> itself.[5]

Webster's defines healing as "to make sound." It might be more accurate if we were to say "to become sound."

Look around! We live in the age of the "nuclear concert," the sound of which will instantly transmute us into light. Are we prepared to listen? I am using nuclear weapons as a very real metaphor for the challenge that faces each of us. This challenge is not so much to do away with nuclear weapons but to transform ourselves to a level of being equivalent to the power of nuclear reality. Our current form, both physical and mental, is inadequate to understand or even cope with the awesomeness around us. We have to incubate a new form, perhaps a formless reforming form. For new music composers, structuring the formless is the challenge of our time. To create a disappearing structure which captivates the mind to witness beyond itself; to be with the unknown, to merge with the unknown, to become the unknown. We must be willing to face our own death in order to live in a new way.

Along the same lines, Stockhausen has said he is writing music, not for the apocalypse, but for the post-apocalypse, for the time of reintegration when people would have to be picking up the pieces. Speaking of his composition "Hymmen" as a physical-psychic therapy he talks of catastrophes to come, and their relationship to increased consciousness. He sees his music as being on the other side of death, on the other side of these coming catastrophes.

> Well, I hear it this way. You see, becoming con-
> scious is already being on the other side. You see

> clearly where we are up to and then death isn't
> frightening any more. Also a collective death is
> large groups. Because you feel that our destiny is a
> universal destiny and not only a terrestrial one. . . . [6]

New healing views matter as consciousness; therefore the assumption that our physical bodies are solid material which eventually decays and dies is no longer valid.

> All matter belongs to the implicate (internal) order
> where everything is alive. "What we call death is
> an abstraction."[7]

Healing is not always comfortable. New-music composers have been severely and unjustly criticized by the traditional medical establishment as well as tonal-classicists. David Tame in his book *The Secret Power of Music — The Transformation of Self and Society Through Musical Energy* devotes a whole chapter to criticizing new-music composers for their lack of consciousness;

> Would the reader allow me here to offer on opinion?
> No proof, no scientific discussion about the pros
> and cons of the conviction I find myself with — just
> a simple gut reaction; that there is something dis-
> tinctly dangerous to the consciousness in such
> music (new music) as this. Dangerous in perhaps
> surprisingly tangible and immediate ways. It is as
> though there exists a chasm within each of these
> compositions: a dark, yawning crevasse which, if
> we allow it to, will gladly swallow up whatever
> portion of our mind we offer it by the directing of
> our attention towards it.[8]

Tame is essentially a man unwilling to change, to let go of his form. A man who does not realize that the very music that he dislikes is challenging him to grow — to become a new person. He is uncomfortable with this music, so he therefore assumes that it has a negative effect on individuals and societies. He wants to go back to a time before the bomb, he wants to "melt" listening to Beethoven. He wants to be spared the pain of transformation. He wants to remain unconscious. Is he that different from you and me?

New music is not a passive experience; it is a way of being. In the words of Boulez:

> Nothing is based on the "masterpiece," on the
> closed cycle, on passive contemplation, on purely

> aesthetic enjoyment. Music is a way of being in the
> world, it becomes an integral part of existence, is
> inseparably connected with it; it is an ethical cate-
> gory, no longer merely an aesthetic one. [9]

In summary, new music is bringing forth necessary changes in our self on both physical and mental levels to be able to live harmoniously in our times and in times to come. We need to listen to and be in touch with the music of our times. New-music composers and musicians need to serve in a very humble way. The days of Beethoven-like power are over. We have to work for and campaign for our audiences — not just for ourselves but for our fellow composers and ultimately for the transformation necessary for a leap in evolution.

A new world is only a new mind!

(William Carlos Williams)

Listen!

Appendix II

BioSonic™ Academy

The BioSonic™ Academy teaches BioSonic™ Repatterning, an energetic approach to music and sound therapy. Classes are offered in cymatics, tuning forks, toning, voice energetics, music listening, mantra, and rhythm. The BioSonic™ Academy also offers classes for professional health care providers integrating BioSonic™ Repatterning into medicine, bodywork, verbal counseling, exercise, and nutrition. Classes are for both lay and professional development.

The following can be ordered through BioSonic™ Enterprises, Ltd.

1. A complete line of tuning forks.
2. Video Tapes including classes and demonstrations.
3. A cassette tape of the interludes in this book: Mind Mist, Mountain Temple and Rain Forest spoken by John Beaulieu with music.

For more information on classes and products write or phone:

BioSonic™ Enterprises, Ltd.
10 Leonard Street #2A
New York, NY 10013
(212) 334-8392

Appendix III

Music Therapy

Music Therapy is a profession which represents the re-emergence of music as a healing force. It's beginnings can be traced back to the observations of a group of professional musicians who worked with returning World War II veterans. The musicians volunteered their time in hospitals, their original intention was to help the veterans pass their time in a pleasurable way. To their surprise the musicians began to notice that the patients who were exposed to music on a regular basis showed an increase in their morale and their socialization skills became better. Their depressions disappeared quicker, as their suppressed emotions found a safe form of expression through music.

The culmination of these original observations and experiences by these musicians became what is now known as the profession of music therapy. During the 1950's and 1960's two professional associations were formed: The National Association of Music Therapy and the American Association of Music Therapy. These associations are now dedicated to understanding the truth about the healing qualities of music and sound. They now include approved university training programs, they certify Music Therapists, support research, and increase the general awareness of the benefits of music therapy. There are currently seventy-six Music Therapy programs in the United States, ranging from the Bachelor of Arts degree to the PhD. level.

Today Music Therapists work in hospitals with special populations which include the mentally retarded, physically handicapped, psychiatric, learning disabled, and those suffering from physical diseases such as cancer and heart problems. There are over 2000 Music Therapists in America serving these populations.

The integration of an energy approach with current music therapy practices is important for the future growth of Music Therapy. Music Therapists have sought to justify the changes they observe in people in terms of behaviorism, emotional release, and more recently through humanistic psychology. Much of their research and philosophical inquiries have tried to fit their experiences into a medical model. The goal is to justify their profession and to prove that it is a valid and accountable part of that system.

Because of this strong emphasis on working within the medical model, Music Therapists are trained in skills which apply to special populations. Their knowledge of how to work with the general public is limited. It is unsual to find a Music Therapist working outside a hospital. Those few who have successfully made this step acquire skill beyond their university training which may involve psychotherapy, guided imagery and bodywork.

I believe the energy approach to sound and music is vital, it offers the professional Music Therapist a new context for their practice. It will enhance their current hospital skills as well as establish a system of observation and feedback of the effects of music on those persons seeking musical help outside a hospital setting.

For example a Music Therapist working with cancer patients can learn to evaluate their patients in terms of the elements. The presentation of elements from patient to patient can be very different even though the medical diagnosis may be similar. The therapist can then recommend musical selections, make a tape, improvise directly with the patient, or even utilize guided imagery with changing elemental voice and/or musical qualities to fit the patient's elemental needs. The doctor and patient do not have to understand the therapist's reasoning just as Music Therapists do not have to understand the doctor's reasoning concerning surgery or chemotherapy. Nor does elemental reasoning have to invalidate humanistic or behavorial goals.

The same skills of elemental evaluation apply in the community. A man who walks slow, talks in a low whispering voice, and complains of heaviness and not enough creativity in his life requires a different approach than a man who walks fast, talks loud, and complains of not sleeping enough. A Music Therapist could use his skills to improvise music to fit their clients' elemental needs, utilize humanistic counseling paying attention to voice changes, and make music listening recommendations. The therapist would be able to monitor the client's progress through elemental observation.

I have written this book for both the lay public and the professional Music Therapist. I believe it is the professional with skills in observing human behavior and assessing that behavior who will be most able to appreciate this approach. The climate within the Music Therapy profession is changing. Many therapists are searching for deeper roots and want to rediscover the ancient power and respect music once held. For them this text offers new possibilities for personal and professional growth. Understanding the energy approach requires a new orientation of thought. Ultimately it requires a new commitment to living. The final result is that all one's skills and philosophy improve, the quality and excitement of living is enhanced.

If you are interested in learning more about Music Therapy you can write to the following professional organizations:

American Association For Music Therapy
66 Morris Avenue
Springfield, New Jersey 07801

National Association For Music Therapy
1133 Fifteenth Street N.W.
Suite 1000 Washington, D.C. 20005

Notes

Listening

[1] Cyril Scott, *Music, Its Secret Influence Throughout the Ages* (London: Theosophical Publishing, 1937), p. 47.

Life Energy

[1] Jonathan Schell, *The Fate of the Earth* (New York: Avon, 1982), p. 11.

[2] Fritjof Capra, *The Tao of Physics* (New York: Bantam, 1984), p. 56.

[3] Donald B. Ardell, *High Level Wellness* (Emmaus, Pa.: Rodale Press, 1977), p. 10.

[4] Ryan and Travis, *Wellness Workbook* (San Francisco: Ten Speed Press, 1981), p. 14.

Elements: The Language of Energy

[1] Dr. Vasant Lad, *Ayruveda: The Science of Self-Healing* (Santa Fe: Lotus Press, 1984), p. 21.

[2] Peter Michael Hamel, *Through Music to the Self* (Wiltshire, England: Compton Press, 1976), p. 94.

[3] Dr. Randolph Stone, *Polarity Therapy* (Reno: CRCS Publications, 1986), p. 34.

[4] Peter Rendel, *Introduction to the Chakras* (New York: Samuel Weiser, 1976), p. 30.

Music and Life Energy

[1] Sufi Inayat Khan, *Music* (New York: Samuel Weiser, 1977), p. 1.

[2] David Reck, *Music of the Whole Earth* (New York: Charles Scribner's Sons, 1977), p. 5.

[3] P. D. Ouspensky, *In Search of the Miraculous* (New York: Harcourt, Brace and World, 1949), p. 122.

[4] Hans Jenny, *Cymatics* (Basel, Switzerland: Basilius Press, 1974), p. 176.

[5] Fritjof Capra, *The Tao of Physics*, p. 56.

[6] Ibid., p. 57.

Voice Energetics

[1] (diagram) Raymond Rizzo, *The Voice As an Instrument* (Indianapolis: Bobbs-Merrill, 1983), p. 1.

[2] Theodor Schwenk, *Sensitive Chaos* (New York: Schocken Books, 1976), p. 126.

[3] (pictures) Hans Jenny, *Cymatics: The Structure and Dynamics of Waves and Vibrations*, Vols. I and II (Basel, Switzerland: Basilius Press, 1967).

[4] Kristin Linklater, *Freeing the Natural Voice* (New York: Drama Book Publishers, 1976), p. 8.

[5] Dr. Morton Cooper, *Change Your Voice: Change Your Life* (New York: Macmillan, 1984), p. 15.

6 Sufi Inayat Khan, *Music*, p. 58.

7 John A. Wheeler and J. Mehra, eds., *The Physicist's Conception of Nature* (New York: Pergamon, 1977), p. 244.

Music

1 Charles Ives, *A Dictionary of Famous Musical Quotations* (New York: Macmillan), p. 83.

2 Dr. Irving Oyle, *The New American Medicine Show* (Santa Cruz: Unity Press, 1979), p. 24.

3 Dr. John Upledger, *Craniosacral Therapy* (Seattle: Eastland Press, 1983), p. 20.

4 Lee Lee Valvoda, *A Dictionary of Famous Musical Quotations* (New York: Macmillan, 1985), p. 68.

5 Joseph Haydn, *A Dictionary of Famous Musical Quotations* (New York: Macmillan, 1985), p. 75.

6 Carlos Castaneda, *The Teachings of Don Juan* (New York: Simon and Schuster, 1968), p. 58.

Tuning Forks

1 (diagram) Gyorgy Doczi, *The Power of Limits: Proportional Harmonies in Nature, Art and Architecture* (Boulder: Shambhala, 1981), p. 97.

2 (diagram) Dr. Randolph Stone, *Polarity Therapy* (Reno: CRCS Publications, 1986), p. 17.

3 Dr. Harold Ives Magoun, *Osteopathy in the Cranial Field* (Kirksville, Mo.: The Journal Printing Company, 1976), Foreword.

4 Ibid., p. 342.

5 Dr. John Upledger, *Craniosacral Therapy* (Seattle: Eastland Press, 1983), p. 25.

6 Manly P. Hall, *The Therapeutic Value of Music* (Los Angeles: Philosophical Research Society, 1955), p. 3.

7 (diagram) McNaught/Callander, *Illustrated Physiology* (New York: Churchill Livingstone, 1983), p. 240.

Mantra

1 Pandit Usharbudh Arya, *Mantra & Meditation* (Honesdale, Pa.: Himalayan Institute, 1981), p. 146.

2 (chart), Ibid., p. 117.

Toning

1 William Stewart, *Environmental Protection Agency*, Pamphlet, 1977.

2 Lester, Sontag, *Environmental Protection Agency*, Pamphlet, 1977.

3 Janet Raloff, "Airport Noise Linked with Heart Disease" (research by Meecham and Shaw), *Science News*, 129:294 (May 7, 1983).

4 E. A. Peterson, "Noise Raises Blood Pressure without Impairing Auditory Sensitivity," *Science*, 211: 1450-2 (March 27, 1981.)

5 Janet Raloff, "Occupational Noise—The Subtle Pollutant," *Science News*, vol. 121: 347-350 (May 22, 1982).

Appendix I

1 Larry Dossy, *Space, Time, and Medicine* (Boulder: Shambhala Press, 1982), p. 75.

2 Ibid., p. 29.

3 John Cage, *Silence* (Cambridge: MIT Press, 1971), p. 34.

4 Ibid., p. 40.

5 Ibid., p. 41.

6 Jonathan Cott, *Stockhausen: Conversations with the Composer* (New York: Simon and Schuster, 1973), p. 77.

7 Larry Dossey, *Space, Time, and Medicine*, p. 90.

8 David Tame, *The Secret Power of Music—The Transformation of Self and Society Through Musical Energy* (New York: Destiny Books, 1984), p. 56.

9 Michael Nyman, *Experimental Music—Cage and Beyond* (New York: Schirmer Books, 1974), p. 23.

Bibliography

Ardell, Donald B. *High Level Wellness: An Alternative to Doctors, Drugs, and Disease*. Emmaus, Pa.: Rodale Press, 1977.

Arroyo, Stephen. *Astrology, Psychology, and the Four Elements*. Reno: CRCS Press, 1975.

Beaulieu, John. "New Music: New Healing": *Ear Magazine*. Vol. 9 Number 3. New York: New Wilderness Foundation, Dec. 1984.

Berstein, Mark. *The Rainbow Book*. Berkeley: Shambhala, 1975.

Blofeld, John. *Mantras: Sacred Words of Power*. New York: E.P. Dutton, 1977.

Bragdon, Clifford. *Noise Pollution—The Urgent Crisis*. Philadelphia: University of Pennsylvania Press, 1971.

Cage, John. *Silence*. Middletown: Wesleyan University Press, 1965.

Capra, Fritjof. *The Tao of Physics*. New York: Bantam Books, 1975.

Cardew, Cornelius. *Scratch Music*. Cambridge: MIT Press, 1972.

Castaneda, Carlos. *The Teachings of Don Juan: A Yaqui Way of Knowledge*. New York: Simon & Schuster, 1968.

Cooper, Dr. Morton. *Change Your Voice: Change Your Life*. New York: Macmillan, 1984.

Copland, Aaron. *Music and Imagination*. Cambridge: Harvard University Press, 1980.

Crofton, Ian and Fraser, Donald. *A Dictionary of Musical Quotations*. New York: Schirmer, 1985.

Cott, Jonathan. *Stockhausen: Conversations with the Composer*. New York: Simon & Schuster, 1973.

Dhiegh, Khigh Alx. *The Eleventh Wing*. New York: Delta, 1973.

Doczi, Gyorgy. *The Power of Limits: Proportional Harmonies in Nature, Art & Architecture*. Boston: New Science Library, 1982.

Dossey, Larry, M.D. *Space, Time & Medicine*. Boulder: Shambhala, 1982.

Easwaran, Eknath. *The Mantram Handbook: Formulas for Transformation*. Petaluma, Ca.: Nilgiri Press, 1977.

Gordon, Richard. *Your Healing Hands: The Polarity Experience*. Santa Cruz: Unity Press, 1978.

Grout, Donald Jay. *A History of Western Music*. New York: W.W. Norton, 1973.

Hall, Manly P. *The Therapeutic Value of Music*. Los Angeles: The Philosophical Research Society, 1955.

Halpern, Steven. *Sound Health: The Music and Sounds That Make Us Whole*. San Francisco: Harper & Row, 1985.

Hamel, Peter Michael. *Through Music to the Self*. Boulder: Shambhala, 1978.

Jenny, Hans. *Cymatics: The Structure and Dynamics of Waves and Vibrations*, Vols. I and II. Basel, Switzerland: Basilius Press, 1967.

Journal of Music Therapy. Washington, D.C.: National Association for Music Therapy.

Katsh, Shelley and Merle-Fishman, Carol. *The Music Within You*. New York: Simon & Schuster, 1985.

Key, Wilson Bryan. *Subliminal Seduction*. Englewood Cliffs: Prentice-Hall, 1973.

Khan, Hazrat Inayat. *Music*. New York: Samuel Weiser, 1962.

Leonard, George. *The Silent Pulse*. New York: Bantam New Age Books, 1981.

Lessac, Arthur. *The Use and Training of The Human Voice: A Practical Approach to Speech and Voice Dynamics*. New York: Drama Books, 1967.

Levarie, Liegmund and Levy, Ernst. *Tone: A Study in Musical Acoustics*. Kent: Kent State University Press, 1980.

Linklater, Kristin. *Freeing the Natural Voice*. New York: Drama Books, 1976.

Magoun, Harold I. *Osteopathy in the Cranial Field*. Kirksville, Mo.: Journal Printing, 1976.

McNaught, Ann B. and Callander, Robin. *Illustrated Physiology*. London: Churchill Livingstone, 1983.

Menuhin, Yehudi and Davis, Curtis W. *The Music of Man*. New York: Simon & Schuster, 1979.

Nyman, Michael. *Experimental Music —Cage and Beyond*. New York: Schirmer Books, 1974.

Oyle, Dr. Irving. *The New American Medicine Show*. Santa Cruz: Unity Press, 1979.

———. *Your Healing Mind*. Millbrae, Calif.: Celestial Arts, 1975.

Ouspensky, P.D. *In Search of the Miraculous*. New York: Harvest Books, 1949.

Pandit, Usharbudh Arya. *Mantra & Meditation*. Honesdale, Pa.: Himalayan International Institute, 1981.

Paynter, John and Aston, Peter. *Sound and Silence: Classroom Projects in Creative Music*. London: Cambridge University Press, 1970.

Pandit, Usharbudh Arya. *Mantra & Meditation*. Honesdale, Pa.: Himalayan International Institute, 1981.

Raloff, Janet. "Airport Noise Linked with Heart Disease" (research by William Meecham and Neil Shaw), *Science News*. 123:294. (May 7, 1983).

———. "Occupational Noise—The Subtle Pollutant." *Science News*. vol. 121:347-350. (May 22, 1982).

Reck, David. *Music of the Whole Earth*. New York: Charles Scribner's Sons, 1977.

Rendel, Peter. *Introduction to the Chakras*. New York: Samuel Weiser, 1974.

Rudhyar, Dane. *The Magic of Tone and the Art of Music*. Boulder: Shambhala, 1982.

Schafer, R. Murray. *The Tuning of the World*. New York: Knopf, 1977.

Schell, Jonathan. *The Fate of the Earth*. New York: Avon, 1982.

Scott, Cyrill. *Music: Its Secret Influence Through the Ages*. London: Theosophical Publishing House, 1937.

Schwenk, Theodor. *Sensitive Chaos: The Creation of Flowing Forms in Water & Air*. New York: Schocken Books, 1976.

Stevens, S.S. and Warhofsdy, F. *Sound and Hearing*. New York: Time-Life Books, 1965.

Stone, Dr. Randolph. *Health Building*. Reno: CRCS Press, 1986.

——. *Polarity Therapy: The Complete Collected Works*. Reno: CRCS Press, 1986.

Tame, David. *The Secret Power of Music*. New York: Destiny, 1984.

Upledger, John E. and Vredevoogd, Jon. *Craniosacral Therapy*. Seattle: Eastland Press, 1983.

Vennard, William. *Singing: The Mechanism and the Technic*. New York: Carl Fischer, 1967.

Zuckerkandl, Victor. *Sound and Symbol: Music and the External World*. Princeton: Princeton University Press, 1969.

Index